A HISTORY

*Ballymena Festival*

1916-2016

**HAZEL BONAR**

Published by Hazel Bonar
©2016 Hazel Bonar
All rights reserved.
ISBN 978-1-5262-0069-3


Designed by April Sky Design, Newtownards
www.aprilsky.co.uk


Printed by GPS Colour Graphics Limited, Belfast

# Contents

# Contents...

# A message from Liam Neeson

As a Freeman of Ballymena, I am always pleased to hear about the good things that are happening in my home town. I want to congratulate Ballymena Festival of Music, Speech and Dance on reaching their centenary year in 2016. Many of my extended family members have been involved over the years in the Festival, whether as teachers or performers or committee members. The Feis has provided a platform for the nurturing of talent over generations and in many areas of the performing arts. I commend the organisers for their hard work and dedication, and I encourage the participants in this special year to appreciate that they are part of a very worthy tradition.

# Foreword by Chairman of Ballymena Festival of Music, Speech and Dance

I consider it a great privilege to be Chairman of Ballymena Festival on the occasion of its Centenary celebrations.

It is only through reading this account of the Festival's history that one realises what a valuable past we have, and what an important part the Festival has played in the life of Ballymena Borough.

When considering how we should recognise our centenary, we felt we should record our past, both by live performances in our Centenary Concert by former competitors, and also in print, so that present and future generations would have a tangible link to the festival history.

We are greatly indebted to Hazel Bonar for undertaking this mammoth task. It has taken many hours to compile the book and we thank the Heritage Lottery Fund for providing the necessary funding for its publication.

It is our sincere hope that Ballymena Festival will continue to provide an invaluable opportunity for local children to perform in front of an audience and, in some cases, as evidenced in this book, go on to achieve excellence in their art.

**Stanley Hughes**
Chairman

'Dedicated to the memory of Marie O'Loan, who loved the Feis.'

# A note from the author

I feel honoured to have been entrusted with the task of researching and writing the history of Ballymena Festival since it first began in 1916. My initial fears that there might not be enough material to fill a book quickly evaporated, and I became fascinated with the stories that emerged from newspaper archives, scrapbooks, photographs and personal narratives. My aim was not just to state the bald facts, but to portray the people who have made the festival happen year after year. Performers, organisers, adjudicators, musicians, volunteers have all combined to make Ballymena Festival what it is today. I also felt that it was important to describe how the festival works in 2016, not just as information for today's readers, but for the benefit of those who come after us, to know who we were and what we did.

I am very aware that as an amateur historian and a novice author, I will have made mistakes, I will have left out stories that might have been told, and I will have forgotten to name names. I apologise in advance.

I have to thank the staff in the local studies department of Ballymena Library for all their assistance and encouragement. Thanks also to Ashleigh Kirkpatrick for her much-valued assistance in image research and information gathering. Andrew Murray, a 2nd year history student at UUC, helped me with research as part of his placement. Members of the Festival Committee tracked down potential contributors and helped with generating interest in the community. Special thanks go to Paddy Wallace and Irene Kingston whose enthusiasm helped to drive the project forward at the very beginning.

I must also thank the publishers, Colourpoint Books, for their help and patience in guiding me through the publishing process.

Publication of this book would not have been possible without the financial support of the 'Sharing Heritage' programme of the Heritage Lottery Fund. I have appreciated the guidance and advice given by their staff.

I must pay tribute to my long-suffering husband, Sam, who has been very supportive of my endeavours. My daughters, Louise and Fiona, have cheered from the side-lines, while friends and family have taken a somewhat bemused interest in the whole process. I thank all of them for their supportive encouragement.

**Hazel Bonar**
November 2015

# Section 1

# The History of Ballymena Festival
# 1916 – 2016

Ballymena Festival

# Ballymena
## 'The Setting'

**B**allymena lies more or less in the centre of County Antrim, advertising itself today as being the Gateway to the Glens. One major geographical feature lies outside the town with Slemish Mountain, once home to the sheep-herding St Patrick, rising gently from the surrounding countryside. In the town itself, the Braid River flows under Harryville Bridge. The waters of the Braid were vital to the establishment and growth of the linen industry in the late nineteenth and early twentieth centuries. The Braidwater Spinning Mill employed over a thousand people at one time and it was only one of several profitable companies that sprang up in Ballymena and the surrounding villages. Ballymena has always been thought of as a shopping or market town and, until the demise of the Fair Hill market in the late 1980s, Saturday was market day for the canny shopper. Equally important but less fragrant trading was carried on in the agricultural markets which served the farming industry. Ballymena was fortunate to have good railway links with other major towns and cities, so goods were ferried in and out with great efficiency. Today, the railway is less important than the road network which services the town, but it still transports passengers to and from their destinations, whether resigned commuter or the more occasional traveller.

The story of Ballymena Festival begins in 1915 when the town's population numbered around 10,000, much smaller than today's total of around 30,000. Ballymena Urban District Council had been formed in 1900 to govern the town. During the week, the people of the town worked hard in their different occupations, many of them in the various mills and factories. On Sundays, the townspeople had their choice of churches and chapels to attend as they wished. The children, happily or otherwise, mostly attended National (later Public Elementary) schools until they were 14, the better off being sent to fee-paying private schools. Health care and welfare provision was under the control of the Ballymena Poor Law Guardians with the workhouse (now the Braid Valley Hospital) being the unfortunate ultimate destination for the very poor and the mentally ill. The Ballymena District Nursing Committee employed nurses to look after patients in their own homes, but should the patient require hospital treatment, they would be treated in the Ballymena District Infirmary now housed in the brand new Waveney Hospital. In 1915, that might have meant being cared for alongside wounded soldiers, since the Waveney was used as an overspill hospital for casualties from the Great War. Read through the local newspapers of the day and see that they were full of casualty lists together with photographs of newly enlisted volunteers, those who had received medals for bravery and the fallen. The town and the country were occupied with a deadly war. Why, at such a time, would anyone want to stage a musical festival?

# 'In the Beginning'

In June 1915, the Ballymena Weekly Telegraph carried a report of a recent meeting.

> *"A largely-attended and representative meeting convened by Mrs Dinsmore of Crebilly Castle was held in Messrs J and R Bell's Hall, Church Street, Ballymena, on Friday evening for the purpose of establishing a Feis Ceoil or Musical Festival for Ballymena. Mr S W Anderson, Ballee, presided and Mrs Dinsmore lucidly explained the objects of the meeting and the advantages to be gained from the formation of the association for the fostering of music in the district, and especially amongst the children of the National Schools. She stated that she had received very general and encouraging promises of support. It was unanimously decided to form the association, and a strong and representative committee was formed to draw up rules etc. in connection with the organisation. Mrs Dinsmore and Mrs Brabazon were elected hon secretaries, Mr Robert MacDonnell, Belfast Bank, hon treasurer and Mr S W Anderson chairman. Those present were afterwards entertained to tea by Mrs Dinsmore and the meeting terminated with the usual vote of thanks."*

The new organisation formed that day was named 'Ballymena Musical Festival Association'. Although the report is relentlessly positive, and indeed the idea of a music festival had received approval from both Protestant and Catholic clergy, there were those who questioned the wisdom of organising music competitions when the country was embroiled in war.

Mrs Dinsmore had not plucked the idea of a musical festival from thin air. The fact was that musical competitions and festivals had been growing in popularity from the end of the 19th century. Welsh Eisteddfods had been in existence for many years, and now similar competitions, without the Welsh language element, began to be organised as Festivals of music. By 1915, the Festival movement had spread quickly throughout the British Isles. In Ireland, Dublin and Cork had taken the lead in organising Feis

Ceoil, while nearer home, Newcastle, Belfast and Coleraine had already started their own Festivals, Coleraine most lately in 1909.

Ballymena, a prosperous town with its satellite villages, was just as capable of mounting a festival as anywhere else and it was almost a matter of civic pride that it should do so. Mrs Dinsmore, second wife of John Dinsmore JP of Crebilly Castle and the Woollen mill in Kells, had attended other festivals and was familiar with the benefits of such a venture. She had a great interest in music and also education and believed passionately that a festival would offer the opportunity to encourage and nurture musical talent. It was Mrs Dinsmore's conviction that the young people of the district, unable to do much to help the war effort, could avoid their musical education being neglected by focusing on competing in the festival. It was also the hope that the platform for talent would help to increase the amount of music that was being taught in schools. At that time, musical education was largely the domain of private teachers and there was a distinct lack of musical infrastructure in education from National School level and beyond. Queen's University in Belfast, for instance, had no chair of music, no choir or orchestra, no music society. Clearly, there was still music being made because, depending on their individual circumstances, the citizens of Ballymena and surrounding districts would have been exposed to music in church, through family music-making, through bands and musical groupings. The aim of the proposed festival was to give a platform for the musically talented to perform and to have their contributions judged by knowledgeable adjudicators.

The Committee, having been elected, set to work to organise the festival, scheduled for May 1916. They set in place the rules of the festival and appealed successfully to the Carnegie Trust for financial aid. The Carnegie Trust sent £10 which helped to defray expenses. In fact, the whole festival in 1916 cost £60 to stage, so the initial investment by the Carnegie Trust was a sizeable one by the standards of the day. Mrs Dinsmore, having been the inspiration behind the idea of a festival, set to work as honorary secretary alongside a Mrs Brabazon. There was much to be done, but the decisions made by that first committee set Ballymena Musical Festival or 'The Feis' on a very sure foundation for the future.

# The Inaugural Festival
## 'Crowded to inconvenience'

The committee of Ballymena Musical Festival Association decided to stage the first Festival on 9th-10th May 1916. Competition was limited to 19 classes in either vocal music or pianoforte. The adjudicator was Dr W G McNaught from England, who encouraged those taking part to enjoy themselves and to learn.

The local newspapers were keen to report on the new festival, and indeed, for many years contained verbatim reports of all that had been said and done. This is part of the report in the 13th May 1916 edition of the Ballymena Weekly Telegraph:-

> "The Inaugural festival under the auspices of the BMFA took place on Tuesday and Wednesday last in Ballymena town hall and proved most successful. For years past it has been generally recognised that, in order to stimulate interest in and encourage the study of musical matters locally, something should be done to bring Ballymena into line with other provincial towns in regard to holding an annual musical festival or competition, which would do much to promote and improve the musical tastes of the community. That the City of the Seven Towers has, in this respect, at last taken its proper place is largely due to Mrs Dinsmore, Crebilly Castle, to whose foresight, energy and organising ability the success of the festival was largely due, and with the assistance of the efficient and hard-working executive committee, the numerous details necessary for the success of an undertaking of this nature were satisfactorily arranged and admirably carried out."

The report goes on to speak about the hope that the Feis would encourage children to want to take part, and that they, in turn, would form the basis of adult competitions in the future. The organisers certainly did all they could to encourage school children to participate, because not only were free lunches provided for school choirs, but the railway organised special trains and reduced fares for competitors and teachers making their way to and from the Festival.

Ballymena Town Hall 1916.
*(courtesy of the Linenhall library)*

In that first year, competitors came from Belfast, Ballymoney, Coleraine, Larne, Portstewart, Whitehead and Dungannon as well as from Ballymena and the surrounding area. The newspapers reported that the Town Hall was completely full all day the first day and that there was 'not the slightest hitch from beginning to end'.

Young Master Walter Lewis DID experience some problems. He was entered in the Piano Solo for under 13 years class and played 'Sweet Dream' by Tchaikovsky, but unhappily for him, although the adjudicator said he had got the feeling of the piece, he could not help remarking that the young pianist was *"considerably handicapped through having his left hand bandaged."* He also pointed out that Walter played the piece *"too slowly but then he was playing at a disadvantage."*

The inaugural festival ended with a prize-winners concert on the Wednesday evening. The adjudicator, Dr McNaught, addressed the audience saying

> *"He hoped all who had attended the two days of the Feis had found them worthwhile for music united them all, clever and dull, and it was non-sectarian. He was there to criticise but if, during the festival, he had said anything to offend anyone, he withdrew it and apologised."*

This was greeted with applause from the audience who had squeezed into the Town Hall for the concert and who were clearly determined to enjoy themselves.

Again, the 13th May 1916 edition of Ballymena Weekly Telegraph paints a vivid picture of the scene,

> *"The Town Hall was crowded to inconvenience by a thoroughly appreciative audience who manifested their approval of the efforts of the prize winning competitors by enthusiastic applause."*

By any standards, the first Festival had been a wonderful success. It had cost £60 to run the Festival but they were able to send £10 profit to the Ladies War Relief Fund for prisoners in Germany.

There was clearly an appetite for a musical Festival in Ballymena, so the Committee settled down to plan for 1917 when Ballymena Feis would be bigger and better.

# Festival Fever
## 'Hatpins and pepper-pots'

In 1917, Dr McNaught returned to Ballymena for the second BMFA Festival. This time, the festival lasted for three days and he was joined in adjudicating duties by Norman Hay. His task was to judge the junior piano competitions while Dr McNaught judged vocal and senior piano classes. A number of years later, the chairman of the festival confided to an opening ceremony audience that there had been some problems in recruiting adjudicators in the war years. He told them about an unnamed adjudicator who was so difficult to persuade to come over to Ballymena, owing to his fear of German submarines in the North Channel, that a stalwart member of the BMFA was despatched to accompany him. On arriving at the adjudicator's house, the terrified judge was still in his dressing gown and was very reluctant to travel. The Ballymena man gave the adjudicator a short time to get ready to come away with him, otherwise 'he would be forcibly taken, dressing gown and all.' Since Dr McNaught and Mr Hay were the only adjudicators during the war, and Norman Hay was based in Coleraine, the finger points at Dr McNaught being the anxious traveller. Fears of submarines must have been dispelled because the now emboldened adjudicator returned twice more to Ballymena in the war years.

The Armistice to end the Great War was signed in November 1918 to general rejoicing. The BMFA Committee probably supposed that with peace would come the opportunity to grow and develop without the backdrop of death and destruction. However, some unexpected events conspired to make the committee stop in their tracks. Mrs Dinsmore, the driving force behind the formation of BMFA, announced that she and her husband were leaving to move to England. To further compound their discomfort, Mrs Brabazon, her fellow honorary secretary, tendered her resignation since she was moving away as well.

Then, in January 1919, the Town Hall burnt down.

To their credit, the BMFA gathered their resources and resolved to carry on, since they were convinced that Ballymena wanted and needed the encouragement of musical talent that the festival offered. Two ladies,

Mrs Wier and Mrs Currie, became honorary secretaries, although Mrs Wier eventually took on all the responsibilities herself. The Town Hall could certainly not be rebuilt in time for the Festival in May, so the competitions were moved to the Protestant Hall on the Galgorm Road. The town council also found a temporary home there. The foundation stone for the new Town Hall, the one which is familiar to us today, was laid in 1924 by the then Duke of York, later King George VI, but it was not officially opened until November 1928.

The Protestant Hall, Galgorm Road
*courtesy of the Linenhall Library*

In the meantime, the Festival grew and prospered year after year. One of the notable developments in these years was the ever increasing number of people prepared to become members of the Association. Their willingness to pay membership fees meant that the Association could afford to be generous in their support of musical education. In 1920, Ballymena became the first musical festival in all of Ireland to offer a bursary as a prize. The committee offered a bursary of 10 guineas for 1 or 2 years to a female voice, living within 7 miles of Ballymena, showing most promise of development. This was won by Miss Hester Bell from Tardree who, as a result of the bursary and also significant financial support from the Dinsmores, was able to attend the Royal Academy of Music. She went on to sing with the Carl Rosa and the O'Mara opera companies. She did not forget Ballymena, however, and returned as guest soloist some years later. She also donated a cup to the festival in recognition of the encouragement that she had been given.

In 1921, a bursary of 10 guineas for male voice was introduced. Great interest was shown and there were 13 entries in that competition. Still more bursaries were added in 1922 resulting in a huge rise in the number of vocal solo entries. Out of 415 entries altogether, 300 were for vocal solos, the greatest number of any musical festival in Ireland.

Singing was certainly high on the agenda in Ballymena and the audiences loved it. By 1923, the festival was lasting a full week with 3 sessions per day. It was calculated that 1500 people had taken part in the competitions, their numbers swollen by the choirs and the soloists taking part in the classes for Mill and Factory workers. The Protestant Hall was simply not big enough to accommodate all those who wanted to cheer on their friends and colleagues. The newspapers reported that hundreds had to be turned away from the Hall because it was already filled to overflowing. The amazing thing was that those hundreds of people, unable to gain admission to the hall, simply waited at the entrance to hear word of who had triumphed. Susan McReynolds, of Braidwater Mill, won a gold medal in the factory/mill solo competition and found herself being carried shoulder high through the streets by exultant crowds. Most of the large mills had their own choirs and they were trained to a very high standard.

The Festival organisers were also keen to encourage singing in the schools, so classes were introduced for choirs from both urban and rural districts. Initially, the numbers taking part were small, but undaunted, some of the committee members took to visiting the schools to persuade them to participate. It was understandable that teachers would be slightly reluctant to become involved, because education

Braidwater Spinning Mill
*This image is reproduced courtesy of the National Museum of Ireland*

was going through a period of change. Until partition in 1920, the National Schools provided compulsory education for children aged 6 to 14. As a result of the Education Act (Northern Ireland) 1923, National Schools were replaced by Public Elementary Schools and Catholic Maintained Schools which were charged with providing education for children aged 4 to 14. The Education Boards which were given the responsibility of effecting the changes were themselves only being established. The majority of these schools had no musical instruments, certainly no pianos, and there was no official compulsion to provide music as a subject. To get around the lack of pianos, many children were taught to sing using the tonic sol-fa method, immortalised in 'The Sound of Music' with the song 'Doe, a deer'. The numbers of schools entering the festival gradually rose until in 1929, there were 29 entries in the school choir section. For a number of years, the Festival arranged for the vocal music adjudicator to conduct a kind of masterclass on the Saturday afternoon of the Festival. All the school choirs sang together, guided and inspired by eminent musicians.

School choirs, mill and factory choirs, village choirs, church choirs, girl-guide and brownie choirs, infant choirs, adult choirs. It seemed that everyone in Ballymena and the surrounding district was singing. Then, one of the adjudicators, Mr Roper, made the suggestion in 1923 that in order to help with diction while singing, the festival should consider introducing Elocution competitions to the syllabus. Accordingly, in 1924, the first classes for Elocution appeared on the syllabus. There were only three classes and 28 entries. That first year the competitors were judged by one of the vocal music judges, Hugh Roberton, founder of the Glasgow Orpheus choir. Thereafter, Elocution would have its own expert adjudicator. It evolved first into being called 'Verse speaking and dramatic interpretation' and eventually into 'Speech and drama' as it is known today.

Ballymena had established itself very quickly on the festival scene, growing rapidly in terms of entry numbers but also in terms of prestige. Other towns took note and they, in turn, formed associations and set up musical festivals. It was the fashionable thing to do. Derry Feis was founded in 1920, Dungannon and Portadown in 1922, Carrickfergus in 1924, Larne in 1925 and Newry comparatively late in 1928.

The newspapers, both local and national, noted these developments and praised the organisation and the ideals of the festival movement. They saw the performance and appreciation of music as being an excellent way of bringing all classes and creeds under the same roof. In 1927, an article in the Irish News stated,

> 'This enthusiasm for music augurs well. It bespeaks a new, more sympathetic, more versatile and more appreciative generation of men and women.
>
> The youths who have been educated to win at Feisanna (festivals) will not believe that musical education begins with 'Dolly's Brae' and ends with 'Derry's Walls' or that 'The Boys of Wexford' is the only song worth singing.'

Of the classes intermingling the same article pointed out:-

> 'A festival brings into pleasant contact people of all classes who, in the ordinary course of events, would probably not be on speaking terms.'

The Belfast Telegraph had earlier reported the enthusiasm of the audience in Ballymena Festival. In 1921, Braidwater Mill had won the Factory and Mill Choirs competition. A local newspaper report had described the scene:-

> 'Tremendous cheering rang out when Braidwater Mill Choir was declared the successful winner. The audience, especially those in the gallery, broke loose and amid tremendous cheering, hats, jackets and handkerchiefs were waved in frantic fashion, whilst hundreds in the body of the hall took up the infection and cheered lustily.'

The Belfast Telegraph commented approvingly, 'Surely it is an achievement to get people roused to that pitch in connection with a musical event.'

The early enthusiasm of the mill and factory choirs did not diminish but rather grew until the competition between them became intense. For their part, the mill owners encouraged the social side of singing and some even kitted out the choirs in matching uniforms. The Braidwater ladies, for instance, wore brown linen dresses with cream collars which had been supplied by the management of the Mill. It is unlikely, however, that the owners would have approved of some of the tactics employed by some of their more fanatical employees. Stories of the intense rivalries have been passed down by festival organisers and choir members alike. It was said that some choir members would have supplies of pepper to shake at their rivals to start them sneezing when they got onstage. Organisers of the Feis learned that it was best to take the winning choir down the back stairs to avoid them coming into contact with hatpin-wielding and embittered contestants and supporters. Newspapers did not report these antics, nor did they comment on the occasion when a winning choir from Belfast had to be given a police escort to the railway station to prevent them being abused by an angry crowd. It was clearly an extraordinary time with tensions and excitement boiling over in overcrowded halls. The Festival had proved that it was not just a platform for the chosen few to show the result of private lessons, instead, it provided the opportunity for people of all ages and social classes to participate and to make music and to be cheered to the rafters by their friends.

# The Twenties

The Festival spent the majority of the 1920s in the Protestant Hall, exiled there while the Town Hall took shape. Every year, the newspaper reports emphasised just how full the hall was, with every available space being taken long before the session was due to begin. In those years, the Festival took place in May, rather than the current February and March. The weather was usually favourable enough for young women to wear their summer dresses, but the disadvantage of a summer festival was that the crowded hall often became unbearably hot and uncomfortable.

Throughout the 1920s the numbers of entries rose steadily - 436 entries in 1923, 455 entries in 1926, 511 entries in 1927. The Festival organisers were delighted that standards were rising at the same time and adjudicators regularly praised the organisation of the Festival and the excellence of the performances they had to judge. Some of those taking part in Ballymena would have appeared in other festivals and, indeed, because Ballymena was comparatively late on the Festival calendar, it was recognised that singers and musicians had the advantage of being judged and critiqued by previous adjudicators so that their performances had the opportunity to be refined and improved. In 1925, a young baritone, Jim Johnston, entered Ballymena Festival with some confidence, having won in festivals all over Ireland. He was taken aback to be told by the adjudicator, E T Davies, that he was not a baritone but a tenor, and a tenor with the possibility of being not just a good local tenor, but a great tenor. The adjudicator denied having the gift of prophecy but he was eventually to be proved right because James Johnston went on to become principal tenor in Covent Garden. (His story is told more fully elsewhere in this history)

In 1926, the Festival took place, as usual, in May. What was less usual was that on the mainland a General Strike had been called by the TUC in support of miners who were facing wage cuts and shorter working hours. Percy Scholes, one of the Festival adjudicators, was making his way to the Festival, but missed the mail boat. Percy was rather resourceful and telegraphed the committee of his plan to hire an aeroplane. Alas, that plan did not come to fruition. Next, he wired the news that he hoped to hire a steam puffer to make the crossing. Again, he had to report failure because there was no coal to be had. Percy Scholes had to be content with a day's delay and a seat on the next available mail boat.

In 1927, the Committee announced that gold medals would no longer be awarded to first prize-winners, but instead, the first place for most classes would earn a solid silver miniature cup. They agreed that if a prize-winner was particularly keen to have a gold medal, they would have it. Silver and bronze medals continued to be given out for second and third place. Occasionally, some classes would have only a silver medal awarded for first place with bronze being given for second and third places. In 1928, Florrie Wallace, later Florrie Collins, came first out of 37 entries for Girls solo, 12 years and under. She achieved 89 marks and although the designated medal for coming first was silver, the adjudicator intervened and requested that she receive a gold medal instead. This was to become her most prized possession throughout her life. She went on to become a music teacher and choir mistress, maintaining her links with the festival through playing piano for traditional dance and also conducting choirs in various competitions.

By the late 1920s, many cups and trophies had been donated to the festival, some of which survive and are used today. Miss Hester Bell, recipient of the first ever bursary, returned to sing as soloist in the 'Accompaniment at Sight' class in 1926 and in 1927 donated a silver cup which is currently awarded for baritone solo.

The Ballymena Observer in May 1927, expressed the opinion that Ballymena Festival was the premier in the north,

> *'Taken as a whole, none of the other festivals can equal in importance or musical prestige the high musical standard of the Ballymena Musical Festival. It is, therefore, little wonder why so many aspirants from far afield compete at Ballymena'*

Hazelbank Public
Elementary School
achieved great success
in 1927

In 1928, the vocal adjudicator, Harvey Green, professed himself to be astonished at the accurate sight-singing of Public Elementary choirs. Compliments were paid to the 'clockwork precision' of the arrangements made by Mrs Wier, the General Secretary. The Festival was praised during the opening of the new Town Hall during a short address by Mr Shaw, Chairman of Urban District Council, on the history and development of Ballymena. He informed the Duke of Abercorn who was performing the opening ceremony that,

> 'The Ballymena Musical Festival Association is doing excellent work in fostering a love of music not only in the town and immediate neighbourhood, but throughout a wide area. The presence of nearly 3000 competitors at the recent Festival indicates the success that has been attained.'

In reply the Duke of Abercorn said,

> 'I am also particularly pleased to note that you do not omit on the aesthetic side the cultivation of music from the programme of your daily lives.'

Committee members and guests mingle
outside the Protestant Hall in 1928

Although the Town Hall opened in 1928, it was not until 1929 that the Festival moved to its new, much more spacious accommodation. The years of cramming into the Protestant Hall were finally over and all could rejoice in the splendour of their new surroundings. That year, the Ballymena Observer reported that there were 847 entries and over 4000 competitors in the various disciplines. The committee had arranged for a new instrumental class, but even the Town Hall was unable to meet its requirements. Instead, those taking part in organ solos competed in 1st Ballymena Presbyterian Church, kindly granted for the occasion.

Ballymena Town Hall was rebuilt and opened in 1928

Since its beginnings, Ballymena Festival had grown and evolved and, to satisfy the enthusiasm of the local dancing fraternity, 1929 saw the introduction of competitions in folk-dancing. These included traditional Irish dancing as well as Scottish country dancing and they were popular straight away with competitors and audience alike. Competitors came from the local area and from further afield. A young Patricia Mulholland travelled from Belfast to compete. She later went on to found the Irish National Ballet and had a huge influence on Irish festival dancing.

The young dancers from Miss McCarley's school are
pictured in the early days of folk-dancing

In the space of a decade, then, the Festival had changed from being wholly devoted to music to incorporating verse-speaking and dance. Yet more changes lay ahead as the Festival faced the coming years.

# The Thirties
## 'Change is inevitable, change is constant' (Disraeli)

In 1930, the chairman of the BMFA, John Woodside JP, died and his successor was Rev W H Sloane, minister of Harryville Presbyterian Church. Unfortunately, Rev Sloane was not well enough to be present for the opening of the new Festival and his duties were performed by Mrs Robert Morton, of Morton's Mills. The Morton Challenge Cup, one of the most prestigious trophies in Ballymena Festival, was donated in this year. It has been keenly contested by aspiring vocalists ever since. Once again, the Town Hall was the venue for most competitions. However, the organ competitions continued to be held at 1st Ballymena church while the YMCA Hall in Wellington Street was pressed into service for some verse-speaking classes.

**YMCA Hall in Wellington Street**
*This image is reproduced courtesy of the National Museum of Ireland*

The YMCA Hall has since been demolished, having stood on the present site of Poundland in the Tower Centre. The Festival had more entries than ever (992) and it now lasted 8 days instead of the original 2 in 1915. Audiences continued to crowd in, festival membership figures continued to be very healthy, and the Festival Committee felt able to give a grant to the newly formed Philharmonic Society to help it grow and develop.

Unfortunately for Rev Sloane, 1931 found him no better, and so the Festival had to carry on without him once again. As always, the newspapers reported the popularity of the various competitions, with people having to sit on the floor of the Town Hall, squeezing in right up to the piano. The consensus of opinion was that the festival movement had been very successful as there had been a definite improvement of musical and cultural standards in the town and villages. One adjudicator, Felix Swinstead, sounded a cautionary note in warning about the possible unwelcome influence of the wireless. He pointed out that people were able to have music 'on tap' and would, therefore, not bother to make music themselves. This was a theme that would be revisited regularly as the years progressed.

Things were looking slightly more cheerful in 1932. Rev Sloane had been for a rest cure and was able to attend the festival. Mrs Dinsmore was unable to be there, but, as was her custom, sent a telegram of good wishes to all. The usual classes were augmented by one for Operatic solo in vocal music, and one for country fiddling. The country fiddling class was included in the instrumental section, although from the very beginning it had a very different format and following. Eventually, though not for many years, it would form the nucleus of what is now known as 'Traditional music'. The evenings for country fiddling competitions were enjoyed greatly for their social aspect as well as for the music.

Rev Sloane did not recover his health and he died in 1933, being replaced as chairman by Rev Robert Strawbridge. Rev Strawbridge was the minister of 1st Broughshane Presbyterian Church, a keen singer himself, and a very skilled organiser. He was to preside as chairman for many years to come, determined to fight off distractions from the wireless in the early days and 'Beatlemania' in later years. (A fuller biography of Rev Strawbridge is given elsewhere in this history.)

Rev Strawbridge, far left, and General Secretary Mrs Wier pictured outside the Town Hall in the 1930s

In 1934, organisers of the Festival were gratified by a 25% increase in entries. There were 1263 entries altogether with a continued very strong showing in vocal music. Over the course of the competitions, 144 choirs took part and there were 465 vocal solos. Singing continued to be extremely popular with participants and performers alike. Nevertheless, other disciplines grew and prospered, notably folk-dancing where the adjudicator, Frank Roche, spent from 9.30 am until almost midnight, judging the jigs and reels. He did have two short breaks, lest anyone think him overworked. Mr Roche was quoted as pleading with the male section of the population to take more interest in folk-dancing and to quit jazz. 'Jazz,' he said, 'is *vulgarity in excelsis.*'

Frank Roche returned the next year, in 1935, to judge the folk-dancing once more. This time, the Festival, celebrating its twentieth anniversary, took place a week later than usual. This was because of the silver Jubilee celebrations for King George V. At the opening ceremony for the Festival, Rev Strawbridge announced the death of Mrs Dinsmore, who had passed away in England. Tribute was paid to the lady who had masterminded the organisation of Ballymena Musical Festival; her work had been taken up and carried on by others who were equally convinced of the value of the Festival movement.

By 1936, the Ballymena Observer was confident enough to state that Ballymena Festival's size and standard outclassed similar provincial festivals. Indeed, visiting adjudicators, many of them eminent musicians and artists in their own right, paid tribute to the standard of the competition and also to the efficiency of the organisation. Yeaman Dodds declared that Ballymena was

> '...a Festival of fellowship. By that I mean that whenever there was a job to be done, there was always someone ready to do it.'

> 'We are full of admiration for the local organisation. We, as visiting judges, ought to pay tribute to the whole of the organisation which was perfectly admirable. If the sessions have been extraordinarily long in some cases, our duties have been lightened by the readiness with which everyone concerned has facilitated us.'

Yeaman Dodds also recalled the performance of a young pianist.

> 'One little girl aged eight played the piano with the artistry of a perfect artist, perfectly naturally...a festival that could bring out

*work like that is doing a great work.*

*Shut off your wireless and give your child a chance! The music a child can make is a million times more wonderful than the finest set on earth.'*

Perhaps it was recalling words like these that led Ruth Wier, the general secretary, to declare at the 1937 AGM of the Ballymena Musical Festival Association:-

*'Every child in Ulster, certainly every child in Antrim, can have their musical powers and their verse-speaking abilities judged and commented on by the very best musicians in the land at a very nominal fee. In this respect, the children of the smallest rural public elementary schools have the advantages coveted by the largest and most expensive boarding schools in the British Isles. Public elementary teachers who appreciate this advantage should be given every encouragement by educational committees and parents.'*

The Festival movement in Northern Ireland had been extremely successful and the Northern Whig wrote approvingly about its influence on the young people of the province.

*'The position which the competitive festival movement has attained in Ulster is a monument to the enthusiasm of organisers, teachers and pupils. It has already exerted a great influence on the cultural life of the Province. Through its impetus young people in particular are developing their talent for the performance of music.... There must exist in Ulster a tremendous reservoir of partly developed musical talent waiting for an appropriate outlet. The music competitions are a splendid training ground for those who are seeking to improve their technique or to catch something of the true spirit of their art. The Festivals are not an end in themselves, but the means to a more perfect flowering of latent genius. Thus considered, they are performing an inestimable service to the Ulster of today and tomorrow.' (Northern Whig 1936)*

While 1936 was a very successful year for Ballymena Festival, 1937 proved to be memorable for all the wrong reasons.

The organisers had decided to run the Festival much earlier than normal in order to avoid clashing with the coronation of the new George VI, brother of Edward VIII, the king who had abdicated in 1936. They also had to take account of the dates of other festivals to avoid clashing with them and so the Festival was set for 29th January until 6th February 1937. Festival organisers, no matter how efficient, have control over neither weather nor viruses and in 1937, both wreaked havoc with the competitions. In the first place, a 'flu epidemic raged in the town throughout January, causing the government to order all public elementary schools to close. Older people were also affected so that throughout the month before the Festival, minimal practising was possible because people were simply too ill to attend practices. To make matters worse, the winter weather was much more severe than usual.

The consequence was that entries were well down in every section except folk-dancing. Folk-dancers must have been made of sterner stuff because entry levels actually rose in their section.

Nevertheless, for the first time in Festival history, the books could not be balanced, and the festival sustained a loss of £124.

1938 had to be better, and it was. Entry levels were higher than ever in all the disciplines with folk-dancing now stretching over two days. Patricia Mulholland's violin playing for folk-dancing was highly commended and the adjudicator professed himself delighted to see so many adults taking part in folk-dancing, something that did not happen so much in the south of Ireland.

For young Mary Murray, 1938 was a very good year because she, a local girl, won the coveted Morton Cup. In a previous competition, the adjudicator had been so impressed with her singing that he recalled her to the platform and asked her to sing once more, saying that her breath control was an example to other competitors at the festival and should be emulated. Many years later, Mary Murray recalled the excitement of winning the Morton Cup. All the singers were held in suspense while the adjudicator made his decision. When it was announced that Mary Murray was the winner, the audience erupted in jubilation and several hefty lads shouldered the successful singer to carry her home in victory.

Mary Murray, later Mrs Barr, was a pupil of Miss Bowen-Evans, a staunch supporter of the Festival, and a gifted music teacher. She had been involved with the festival from the very beginning and trained numerous choirs, vocalists and musicians during her association with the festival. (A fuller biography appears elsewhere in this history) Mary Murray became a well-known music teacher herself and continued to support the festival.

And so to 1939, the last festival of the decade and the last festival before the outbreak of war in September of that year. It was impossible to miss the signs of war looming. The newspapers reporting the Festival also carried details of air-raid warnings and even in the reporting of the Festival, the newspapers could not resist making reference to what was happening elsewhere.

Mary Murray with the Wier silver potato ring

*'Once again we are in the middle of Feis week in Ballymena. Hitler, for once, has to take second place, in fact he has been almost forgotten and music lovers and dancers from far and near have devoted themselves to a time of pleasant rivalry and good fellowship.'*

Ballymena counted itself fortunate to have maintained excellent attendances and interest in the Festival. The newspapers pointed out that other centres had seen interest falling away but entry levels for all disciplines were still very high in Ballymena. Folk-dancing continued to grow with between 400 and 500 entries out of a total entry of over 1200 but the best attendance of the Festival was on the Thursday evening when the Town Hall was packed out with an audience eager to hear Operatic Solo, the Boal Cup competition, Ladies and Mixed voice choirs and Senior song and chorus.

Verse-speaking had been growing steadily over the years since 1924 when the committee had added it as 'Elocution' to help singers with their diction. Tyrone Guthrie had been adjudicator in 1927, 1928 and 1934. He went on to be a leading theatrical director, knighted in 1961 for services to theatre. He adjudicated in Ballymena as a young man at the beginning of his distinguished career. In contrast, Laurence Binyon, who adjudicated

33

in verse-speaking in 1939, was nearing the end of a distinguished career as poet and writer, having been Professor of Poetry in Harvard in 1933-1934. He will always be remembered, though, for having written 'For the fallen' in September 1914. The words will be familiar since they are used in Remembrance Day services.

'They shall not grow old as we who are left grow old
Age shall not weary them, nor the years condemn.
At the going down of the sun and in the morning
We will remember them.'

There is a poignancy in the knowledge that the words he wrote would be relevant to so many more people over the coming years of the 2nd World War.

After war was declared in September 1939, the organisers of Ballymena Festival decided that it would be impossible to continue and so, until 1946, the Festival was suspended.

# After The War
## 'The time of the singing of the birds is come'

Monday 8th April 1946 saw the opening of Ballymena Musical Festival after its enforced absence during the war years. The chairman, Rev Strawbridge, made his customary speech at the opening ceremony.

*'If I were expected to preach a sermon this afternoon I should have no difficulty in finding an appropriate text. It would be 'The winter is past, the flowers appear upon the earth; the time of the singing of the birds is come' (Song of Solomon 2 v 11)*

*In a few weeks' time it will be exactly 7 years since we held our last Musical Festival. Some 4 months after that Festival (May 1939), winter descended upon the earth in the shape of War. The nation was mobilised for Total War. Many things which we had come to look upon as part and parcel of our everyday life had to be abandoned because of the stress and strain due to war conditions - and amongst other things, our annual Musical Festival.*

*Whilst we realize that the decision to abandon our Festival in war time was a wise one - in fact it would not have been possible to have carried on - still, as the years passed, many people began to feel increasingly that the lack of our annual competitions was a distinct loss to the musical and cultural life of the community. I am of the opinion that the standard of appreciation of music suffered considerably. And many promising young vocalists and instrumentalists might have developed into really good artists if they had had the incentive to continue their musical education and the objective which the annual competitions supplied.*

*Anyhow, the winter of war has passed, the time of the singing of birds has come again and it is a great delight to us all that that is so.'*

Rev Strawbridge also had to announce the changing face of the committee. In June 1945, when the BMFA gathered to plan the post-war Festival, Mrs Wier tendered her resignation as General Secretary. The Treasurer also resigned, leaving the committee with the difficult task of regrouping and rebuilding. Mrs Wier had been such an energetic and pivotal secretary that it was only with the greatest reluctance that the committee accepted her declaration that she simply could not shoulder the burden once again. Mr James Owens took on the role of General Secretary so capably performed by Mrs Wier. She continued to be a valuable member of the Association for many years to come. (A fuller biography of Mrs Wier is found elsewhere in this history.)

To return to 1946, the first post-war Festival began with over 1000 entries and the organisers were delighted to welcome back as instrumental music adjudicator, Mr David Yacamini, who had endeared himself to Ballymena on previous visits. The vocal music adjudicator was a Mr B M Lewis who complimented highly the work of Miss Bowen-Evans. The newspapers reported his remarks,

> 'The singing of the Linenhall choir was very charming, and he was indebted to the very gracious and talented lady who conducted them for the work she had put before him all that week. He deeply appreciated it because she was one of those people who were doing such a lot of good work for music in this country.'

Miss Bowen-Evans also saw great success with her instrumental pupils, going on to win the Meta Wilson Cup for teachers with most successes in the instrumental section.

Miss Bowen-Evans pictured in her music studio

Sadly, Miss Bowen-Evans was already ill and she made the decision to retire and return to her native Wales. A party in her honour was held in October 1946 and she thanked the people of Ballymena for their friendship and kindness to her.

Edith Bowen-Evans died 2nd February 1947 and Rev Strawbridge announced her death at the opening ceremony of the festival later that year:-

*'Perhaps there was no one person who did so much, on the musical side, to achieve the objects we have in view and to raise the standard of our annual Festival to the high position which it has attained. Throughout the whole history of the Ballymena Festival Association the pupils and choirs of Miss Bowen-Evans played a large part in our annual festivals. She was a true artist and could not be satisfied with anything short of the very best. The high standard of attainment reached by her pupils and choirs made them worthy competitors at any Festival, and they not only carried off many prizes each year but also did much to raise the standard of the competitions to a high level. Her death is a grievous loss to the world of music but the influence of her work will long abide.'*

(A fuller biography of Miss Bowen-Evans is given elsewhere in this history.)

In 1948, a Perpetual Cup for choir competition was presented in memory of Miss Bowen-Evans. Her role as conductor of the Linenhall choirs was taken over by Goodlett Leetch and the choirs continued to be an important part of Ballymena musical life for many years.

The Festival was always willing to introduce new disciplines and in 1948, classical ballet competitions were staged for the first time. However, entries generally were down considerably on pre-war figures with 852 entries overall. Folk-dancing was especially affected with just over 200 competing. The standard of individual dancing suffered, although team dances were praised by the adjudicator.

By 1949, things were beginning to look more positive with a renewed vigour and enthusiasm apparent among the committee members. Mr James Owens had realised that the role of General Secretary was simply too much for one individual and, following his resignation, the committee made the wise decision to divide the work and to appoint section secretaries. From then on, the section secretaries made the necessary arrangements for their particular discipline, while the General Secretary took on more of an overseeing and coordinating role.

The folk-dancers returned in large numbers with over 600 entries out of an overall 1355 and, to the delight of the committee, the town hall was packed once more for the choir competitions. One of these competitions was to see which choir would represent Northern Ireland at national level in London for the Festival of Britain in 1951. All in all, the feeling was that the festival was beginning to be like its old self once more. A newspaper article reflected on the difficulties that the association had faced in starting again after the war, pointing out that a new generation had grown up. The stress and strain of six years of conflict had left its mark on those who had been so enthusiastic before then, and among the public there was a general waning of interest in musical festivals. Ballymena Musical Festival Association also had to cope with the rebuilding of the committee from the foundation up. Nevertheless, the organisers must have felt that they had weathered the storm and could look forward with confidence to a new decade.

# The Fifties
## 'Is Ballymena Festival on its way out?' Ballymena Observer, February 1957

The new decade began brightly enough for Ballymena Festival with several new cups being presented, an increase in entry numbers, and the decision to revive the prize-winners concerts at the end of competitions. The concert for the junior prize-winners took place on the Friday afternoon of the Festival with the seniors performing in the evening. This was a glamorous affair with evening dress being worn and the honorary accompanist, Miss Dorothy Kelly, from London, wrapped in furs.

The winner of the Morton Cup in 1950 was Helen Sloan, who received high praise from the adjudicator. Dr Robson said that her rendition of 'The Linden Tree' was one of the most beautiful productions of it he had heard for many years.

Although the standard of vocal music remained very high, it is clear that, by this time, folk-dancing had become by far the biggest section in the Festival. Some of the classes were huge with at least one class having over 100 entries. The poor adjudicator only coped by judging the dancers 2 or 3 at a time. The ballet adjudicator did not have the same problem because numbers were not large, although the standard was said to be high. Ballet competitions eventually finished in 1952.

In 1951, the Festival decided to invite a guest speaker to begin proceedings on the opening day. Mrs Haughton, from Cullybackey, declared that,

> 'In this mechanical age, people are all too prone to derive their entertainment from machine made products. The Feis does a wonderful thing in encouraging people to do something for themselves. It is a wonderful antidote to mechanical entertainment such as radio.'

In a further departure from tradition, the Festival now presented prize-winners with new medals finished with bronze. These medals had been designed by Martin Tallents, the choir director from Braidwater Mill. The distinctive medals featured the name of the section in which the prize was awarded.

Martin Tallents seen here in the centre back row

The choir nights were no longer attracting huge audiences and, indeed, the number of choirs entering the festival was greatly reduced. Nevertheless, the adjudicator enjoyed the 'Senior Song and Chorus' when former members of factory choirs got together as 'The Old Stagers' and made music once again.

Ballymena Festival had mostly been held in May, occasionally earlier in the year, but in 1952, the decision was taken to move the festival to begin in February. A sense of sadness pervaded the opening of the Festival because the King, George VI, had died just six days before, and a minute's silence was observed. It had been intended that the NI Minister of Education, Rt. Hon Harry Midgeley, would speak at the opening ceremony, but he was unable to attend because it was customary for cabinet ministers not to undertake public engagements until after the late monarch's funeral. Rev Strawbridge spoke instead, and it was his sad duty to announce the deaths of several founder members of the Association. These included George Bellis, Mrs Currie, John Kirkpatrick, conductor of the Seven Towers Choir, as well as R J Craig who as principal of Hazelbank School had enjoyed much success with his pupils at the Festival.

On a happier note, several new cups were presented. Folk-dancing continued to break all records, with 940 entries out of a total of 1634. Dr

Havelock Nelson was the adjudicator in music, although it should be pointed out that even by 1952, only piano and violin featured in instrumental competitions.

Dr Havelock Nelson returned again to adjudicate in 1953. This time, Rt. Hon Harry Midgeley, NI Minister of Education, was able to attend to speak at the opening ceremony. However, a shadow of sadness was cast once more because of the Princess Victoria disaster on 31st January. A minute's silence was observed for the victims of the tragedy. In his speech, Harry Midgeley talked about his strong desire to see the establishment of a school of music for Northern Ireland. The cost of such a project was prohibitive at that particular time, but it was his hope that it would soon be possible to proceed. He spoke of having gained the support for his project from the NI Minister of Finance, Maynard Sinclair, but alas, he was one of those who had perished in the Princess Victoria disaster. He was determined, he said, to pursue the idea of a music college with Sinclair's successor as Minister of Finance.

In the meantime, he extolled the virtue of music as being a force for good in establishing a better and more peaceful world. He congratulated the organisers and declared that Ballymena was one of the best festivals in the province and was probably more distinctive than most.

Entries continued to rise in all disciplines except music, and in verse-speaking, the organisers introduced a new class for extempore speaking for adults. This proved to be very popular with participants and audience alike.

In 1954, the Festival invited Captain Terence O'Neill to be the guest of honour at the opening ceremony. Captain O'Neill, at that time deputy Speaker of the House of Commons at Stormont, told the audience that Dublin was no longer the artistic centre of the island because great strides had been made over the past 50 years to spread the appreciation of music and the arts in Ulster.

The appreciation of culture went against the general stereotype of the Ulsterman:-

> *'People in the north were supposed to be dour and industrial and interested in nothing that did not bring some profit.'*

He commended the growth of public speaking among the young and congratulated those who took part in the adult extempore speaking classes.

As if to underline that Ballymena had played a role in the cultivation of the arts, the Traditional dance adjudicator, George Leonard, later said that since he first came to Ballymena 15 years before, standards had improved out of recognition. He also drew attention to the importance of proper dress to enhance the artistry of the performance.

By 1955, the Festival turned to the world of horticulture and invited Guy Wilson to speak at the opening ceremony. The renowned daffodil breeder confessed to being a music listener rather than a creator or performer. Nevertheless, he saw that the love of music transcended national borders and religions. Recalling the fact that John McCormack had first been discovered at Dublin Feis, Guy Wilson spoke of attending a concert given by the famous tenor in the Ulster Hall. The audience represented many shades of political opinion, but that night '*There was no border.*' He was rather less tolerant of some of the new forms of music-making, declaring that crooner and jazz band music was '*monkey-house entertainment.*'

There were many highlights during the 1955 Festival. Patricia Mulholland was singled out for praise with her fiddle playing during the folk-dancing. One of her dancing disciples, Norman Maternaghan, who had begun his dancing career attending Irish dance classes in the Protestant Hall on Saturday mornings, had himself progressed to forming his own dance troupe. The adjudicator awarded first prize in the reel for couples over 17 years to his team, declaring that '*this couple could*

Lily Agnew, Agnes Grey and Norman Maternaghan
outside the Town Hall

*take their place anywhere in the world of dancing.*' By popular demand, Norman Maternaghan himself performed an exhibition dance. Norman

Maternaghan made his career in dancing, changing his name to Norman Maen and working all over the world as a dancer and choreographer.

Another local girl who made headlines in the Festival was Lily McCready of Summerfield Street. A talented young vocalist, she was awarded the highest marks of the Festival for her Scots Song (a splendid 94 marks awarded) and 91 for her performance in Moore's Melodies. However, because she was six weeks too young for the qualifying age, she could not be awarded the cup for either competition. In addition, she was too young to be eligible for entry to the Morton Cup. The adjudicator, Helen Henschel, said in appreciation of her,

> 'Just a little slip of a girl is Miss McCready and I do not think she has the slightest idea of how beautifully she sang.'

The organisers were disappointed that Lily could not be awarded the trophies but felt that it was important to abide by the rules. She returned the next year in 1956 and this time was awarded the Hood cup for soprano solo.

The guest speaker at the opening of the 1956 Ballymena Festival was Mrs Marie Trimble, from Enniskillen. She was a music teacher and wife of the editor and publisher of 'The Impartial Reporter', but her chief claim to fame was to be the mother of Joan and Valerie Trimble, famous piano duettists. The Festival was rather later than usual, mainly because the association was keen to avoid the worst of the winter weather, however, they had chosen dates which clashed with Belfast Festival. Entries in music were down as a result. There were some excellent performances from those who did attend and the music adjudicator, Dr Hutchinson, singled out Heather Livingston (later Clarke) for special praise. She was, he said, 'an artist in the making.' She was the winner of the class for senior pianoforte solo.

The Linenhall choirs had continued to win prizes under the direction of Goodlett Leetch and they received a great deal of praise. However, in the Morton Cup competition, the adjudicator felt that the correct standard of singing had not been achieved, and, consequently, withheld the cup.

There were no such problems in the folk dancing with huge numbers of participants and a very high standard of performance. Tillie Burnett and Agnes Grey received 99 marks for their senior double jig, an extraordinary feat.

The province had suffered an electricity strike during the festival, but although much of the country was plunged into darkness as a result, in Ballymena Town Hall, the retention of a gas lighting system meant that classes could continue as normal.

Poor audience numbers for the festival were beginning to be of major concern to the organisers. Rev Strawbridge was disheartened that people were not prepared to make the effort to attend the festival and support the participants.

This feeling of being disheartened carried on into the next year, causing the Ballymena Observer to wonder in its headline, 'Is Ballymena Musical Festival on its way out?' There was no guest speaker for the opening ceremony and, in fact, this was never revived, instead relying on whichever adjudicator was available to make some opening remarks. Folk dancing and verse speaking had strong entries but music entries were down once again. In a bid to avoid the embarrassment of the Morton Cup being withheld as in the previous year, the organisers decided to revert to a format where adjudicator marks awarded to the winners of qualifying classes were not revealed at the time. The highest mark awarded guaranteed the Morton cup for the successful singer. The format may have ensured that the Morton cup was awarded, but it deprived the audience of the chance to hear the singers in competition with each other.

In his closing remarks for the 1957 Festival, Rev Strawbridge, as chairman, dared to voice the disappointment of the committee and he wondered if, with such poor audiences compared to previous years, it was worth carrying on. Any successful festival needed to have good adjudicators, good competitors and good audiences who served to give the performers the extra impetus to perform well.

Thankfully, the committee did not succumb to the temptation to wind up the Festival. In 1958, Rev Strawbridge had completed 25 years as chairman, a feat unequalled in the province, and a presentation was made to him to mark the occasion. Mrs Wier, the former General Secretary, paid tribute to him and to his continued service to the association over so many years. She spoke of his love of music, his great gift of organisation, his fondness for children and his patience in performing the miracle of getting so many choirs on and off stage with military precision.

Mrs Wier presents a gift to mark Rev Strawbridge's
25 years as chairman

The festival now lasted over two weeks and, considering that the chairman considered it necessary to be present for much of the time, this represented a feat of endurance and patience for the Rev Strawbridge. Country fiddling nights regularly went on after midnight, as did the senior men's chorus.

Arthur Reckless was the adjudicator for vocal music and he was delighted by the standard of the choirs he heard. After junior hymn singing he declared,

> *'If I were the most irreligious man in Ballymena, I think tonight I would have been converted.'*

He also praised the High Kirk choir under the direction of Harold Alexander,

> *'I do not know how the conductor managed to get such effects, undoubtedly he had got something, for he stunned us all.'*

By 1959, the organisers of the Festival had decided to be more proactive and a small publicity committee had been formed. They had done their best to let people know about the festival in

Harold Alexander is pictured
standing back row, far right

the hope that audience figures would improve. The Council had again awarded a small grant to help with expenses. Entries hovered around the 1500 mark. There was no doubt that young performers wanted to participate in the Festival, but it seemed that for too many Ballymena people, attendance at Ballymena Festival was no longer the attractive prospect it had once been.

# The Sixties
## 'For the times, they are a changin' (Dylan)

The sixties are generally viewed as being a time of change, of dissatisfaction with the old order and a desire for new ideas. How would the Festival fare in the face of pop music, experimental art and even civil disturbances?

The Counties Antrim and Derry Fiddlers Association wanted no truck with pop music since they were dedicated to encouraging interest in traditional fiddling. Country fiddling had long been on the syllabus of the Festival and in 1960, the Fiddlers Association presented a cup in memory of Charles O Curry. He had been to the forefront of the drive to promote traditional fiddling. Country fiddling was traditionally held on the Friday evening of the Festival. As always, it entailed a late night, but the large audience was delighted with the music.

The traditional dancers were happy to continue with their jigs and reels and their adjudicator, Mona Scully, praised Ballymena as being 'the dancing town'. Over 4 days, she adjudicated 800 entries and declared that she had enjoyed the happy atmosphere.

Verse-speaking had seen a rise in entries and Mrs Taggart, the adjudicator implored those taking part to retain their own way of speaking. Successive adjudicators had emphasised that Oxford English was not required:-

> 'Never be ashamed of where you come from. Good speech training will never, never spoil your own intonation. We don't want you all to be patterns of someone else. We want you to speak with individuality, with your own intonation, but clearly and distinctly.

There had also been a rise in music entries, and hopes were high that audience figures would be healthier than of late. The weather, however, was to cause problems with heavy snow falling during the week. Rev Strawbridge remarked that one boy sang a song containing the line:-

> 'I snap my fingers at the snow.'

He was glad that most competitors had done that, unfortunately, the same could not be said for potential audience members.

In the following year, 1961, the music adjudicator, Leslie Regan, touched upon another reason for poor audiences. He commended the volunteers and organisers for the festival for holding the fort,

'..until the present desire for television lessened'

In June 1962, an old friend of the festival, Mrs Wier, was awarded MBE for public service in Ballymena. (A fuller account of her life and work is given elsewhere in this history.)

The winter of 1962 - 1963 was especially severe with the worst snowfall since 1947. Blizzards in early February caused the glens to be cut off and newspaper reports featured helicopters taking supplies to the stricken districts. Ballymena managed to keep streets open, despite heavy snowfall on 12 February.

In a departure from tradition, the country fiddlers were now joined by new instrumentalists. Classes were introduced for piano and chromatic accordions and together they formed the new 'Traditional Music' section. As before, the competitions were held on the Friday evening and the music continued into the small hours.

Rev Strawbridge retired from active ministry in Broughshane, having served the congregation faithfully for 43 years. He remained as chairman of the Festival, however, declaring that he had come to realise that it was worth continuing with the Festival for the sake of the many children who were involved in competition. He felt that it was important that they should have a taste of the joy that the performing arts could bring.

The organisers of the Festival decided that the instrumental section ought to have greater variety, and in consequence, piano and violin, the old faithfuls, were joined by junior recorders, junior string orchestra and flutes with the possibility of a brass section being added the next year. The adjudicator for instrumental music in 1964, Dr Melville Cooke, was highly impressed by the skill of those playing flute. After senior solo he said, '*I am really amazed at the degree of achievement these performers have achieved.*' Ballymena Young Conquerors Band (A) and (B) took part in the flute quartet class and he confessed that he had never heard a flute quartet perform before.

Ballymena Young Conquerors pictured in the minor Town Hall
*Image reproduced with permission of Ballymena Young Conquerors*

The folk-dancing section had over 1000 entries in 1964, and respectable entries in all other sections. And yet, to the consternation of the organising committee, the Festival's costs had been over £700, and they were, yet again, not able to balance the books. It was not a significant figure (£3 in the red) but it caused executive committee members Dr Robert and Mrs Dorothy Simpson to raise the question of what might happen in the future if frost or fog interfered badly with the Festival and they were left with really big losses. At their suggestion, Gallaher Limited was approached to see if they would help with sponsorship. Gallaher's agreed and gave £100 to the Festival. Their generosity continued for years to come and enabled Ballymena Festival to present bursaries in the various disciplines. Incidentally, Mrs Dorothy Simpson had grown up with the Festival, not just because she had taken part in the music competitions but because she was one of Rev Strawbridge's daughters. She was a teacher in Ballymena Academy, her husband, Robert, was a local GP, who for a number of years had been involved in local politics. Together, they took a huge interest in the Festival, serving in various capacities.

In 1965, the success of the newly established flute classes encouraged the festival organisers to include classes for brass instruments. These were for solo, quartets and ensembles and in this first year, Ballymena Silver Band supplied all the competitors. By 1966, the sponsorship from Gallaher's had enabled bursaries to be offered in vocal solo, choral, instrumental, verse-speaking and dancing classes. The biggest audiences continued to be in the traditional music section and Rev Strawbridge proclaimed his satisfaction at seeing such an interest,

*'It is a great thing in these days of Beatlemania and all other manias of that sort, to see that there are so many folk interested in traditional music, which I think is so well worthwhile.'*

In 1967, the traditional musicians found themselves in the company of yet more new instrumentalists. John McGarvey was a very keen banjo player and teacher and, thanks to his influence, banjo classes were introduced to the Festival's traditional music syllabus. The banjos became popular very quickly and entries for these classes remained healthy for a number of years to come.

In 1968, Rev Strawbridge decided to retire as chairman of the

John McGarvey is pictured playing banjo with his daughters

Festival. He had been chairman for 35 years, and as he pointed out himself, had never expected to serve for that length of time. He was presented with engraved cufflinks by the grateful committee who invited him to become the first President of Ballymena Musical Festival. His successor as chairman was Raymond Marshall, a local man who had been steeped in music from an early age. His association with the Festival went back to his first appearance in 1929 as a boy soprano. He also played piano and had great success in tenor classes in Ballymena Festival and elsewhere. As a former pupil of the celebrated teacher, Miss Bowen-Evans, Raymond Marshall represented both the past and the future of the Festival.

Raymond Marshall competed regularly at Ballymena Festival

Much had been accomplished in the 1960s to encourage the teaching and enjoyment of instrumental music in County Antrim schools. F Malcolm Fletcher, a charismatic Englishman, had been appointed County Music Adviser earlier in the decade, and with great flair and energy, he set about introducing musical instruments into schools and ensuring that tuition was made available. Many children sounded their first musical notes using a descant recorder while some took up more complicated orchestral instruments. One of the results was that the Festival now saw the need for further creation of classes to allow the young instrumentalists to compete together. Classes for junior and senior string, brass, woodwind and orchestra were established and even the humble recorder was pressed into competition with classes for recorder groups.

Times had certainly changed in the sixties and yet, as the seventies drew near, the Festival continued to face an uncertain future.

# The Seventies
## 'There may be trouble ahead' (Berlin)

As the seventies got under way, the local newspapers continued to highlight the excellent work done by the volunteers who kept the Festival going. This contrasted sharply with the apathy shown by potential audiences. In one rather scathing Ballymena Observer article in 1970, a journalist criticised the lack of support shown by the majority of the people in the town, sometimes by even the parents of those taking part. This was, of course, so very different to the early days of the Festival, when members of the press practically had to fight their way through the crowds to get to the press table. These days, as some adjudicators had remarked, people were having to perform to rows and rows of empty seats.

This was not, however, a problem confined to Ballymena Festival, and adjudicators who did the rounds of the Festivals in Northern Ireland and Britain, reported that similar situations were happening everywhere.

In 1971, thanks to decimalisation, the old shillings and pennies were replaced by pounds and new pence. Everyone braced themselves for financial meltdown and rising prices, while Raymond Marshall, as chairman, took the opportunity to advertise how cheap it was to come to the Festival. The Traditional dancing section welcomed some dancers from Buncrana, Co Donegal, the first time there had been cross-border entries from the dancing fraternity. In 1972, the traditional dancing section faced some competition from a breakaway Nine Glens Festival. The fear had been that this would adversely affect the numbers competing in Ballymena. Numbers, however, were only slightly down with 1600 entries.

1974 was probably a year to forget for Ballymena Festival in that, if anything could go wrong, it did. All the arrangements had been put in place for the usual dates in February, but just as the organisers had no control over weather or viruses, so they discovered, they had no control over politics either. On 7th February 1974, Edward Heath, the Conservative Prime Minister, called a snap General Election. The election was to take place on 28th February. In those days, the Town

Hall was used to count votes so it was not going to be available for either Traditional Music or Dancing. Programmes had already been printed for the Festival but they had to be scrapped and new ones printed.

The decision was taken to postpone the dancing and traditional music until May, that being the earliest date that the Town Hall was free for five consecutive days. New adjudicators had to be found as the previous ones were unable to come for the new dates.

Things still did not go smoothly and the organisers were constantly bedevilled by 'difficult circumstances.' The week in May chosen by the organisers happened to coincide with the Ulster Workers Council strike. The resulting power cuts meant that the hall was left without light for long periods. Classes held in the evening had to be rushed through before daylight faded so that whereas the 'Big Night' normally ended well after 11.00 pm, this year it finished at 9.00 pm. There had been a record entry for the festival, with over 2400 entries received, but the general unrest of the period meant that many entrants stayed at home. Those who made it to Tuesday evening at the Town Hall were treated to a bomb hoax, necessitating the evacuation of the entire building. After a police search which found nothing untoward, dancing resumed.

Those who took part in the Traditional Music competitions also had problems because of petrol shortages and the power crisis. The evening session was supposed to get under way at 7.30 pm but it was after 8.00 pm before they began. The lights came on shortly afterwards and stayed on for the duration of the evening with the competition not finishing until well after 11.00 pm.

Apart from nerves being shattered, one of the unwelcome results of the 1974 difficulties was that the Festival, once again, was in financial difficulties. In 1975, Raymond Marshall, in speaking to the press, emphasised that inflation was having a damaging effect with prices constantly rising. The cost of staging the Festival had now risen to £1300 with miniature cups doubling and medals tripling in price. Town Hall rent had risen by 20%. The Borough Council initially offered £100 to help with the situation and this was eventually raised to £250, for which the Committee was very grateful.

Despite the problems caused behind the scenes by money worries, the standards of the performers who came along remained very high. It is interesting, with hindsight, to look back on some of the names who have become very well-known outside of Ballymena Festival. Class

28 Boys' Vocal Solo is a case in point. James Nesbitt, Broughshane, competed against Martin O'Hagan and David Delargy of Garron Tower. Eventually, Martin and his brother Eugene would join with David Delargy in concerts and recording contracts as 'The Priests'.

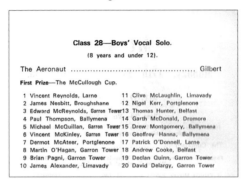

**Class 28—Boys' Vocal Solo.**

(8 years and under 12).

The Aeronaut ............................................ Gilbert

First Prize—The McCullough Cup.

| | |
|---|---|
| 1 Vincent Reynolds, Larne | 11 Clive McLaughlin, Limavady |
| 2 James Nesbitt, Broughshane | 12 Nigel Kerr, Portglenone |
| 3 Edward McReynolds, Garron Tower | 13 Thomas Hunter, Belfast |
| 4 Paul Thompson, Ballymena | 14 Garth McDonald, Dromore |
| 5 Michael McQuillan, Garron Tower | 15 Drew Montgomery, Ballymena |
| 6 Vincent McKinley, Garron Tower | 16 Geoffrey Hanna, Ballymena |
| 7 Dermot McAteer, Portglenone | 17 Patrick O'Donnell, Larne |
| 8 Martin O'Hagan, Garron Tower | 18 Andrew Cooke, Belfast |
| 9 Brian Pagni, Garron Tower | 19 Declan Quinn, Garron Tower |
| 10 James Alexander, Limavady | 20 David Delargy, Garron Tower |

Vocal Class 28 in 1975 had some
illustrious participants

In 1976, the Festival celebrated its diamond anniversary.

***Programme***

for

*The Diamond Jubilee*

(1916—1976)

of

**BALLYMENA MUSICAL FESTIVAL
ASSOCIATION**

Affiliated to British Federation of Music Festivals

1976

TOWN HALL, BALLYMENA

**MUSIC**

MONDAY, 16th FEBRUARY—SATURDAY, 21st FEBRUARY

**VERSE SPEAKING**

TUESDAY, 17th FEBRUARY—SATURDAY, 21st FEBRUARY

PRICE 30p

Front cover of the programme
for 1976

Local papers devoted more space than usual to tell the story of the Festival's growth and development, drawing attention to some of the characters who had been involved during its history. The Festival itself ran smoothly with excellent performances and the usual high standard of organisation. There was a sad ending in that one of the music adjudicators, Mr Arthur Rooke, who had enjoyed his time immensely in Ballymena, became ill at the airport while on his way home. He was taken to the Massarene Hospital, then transferred to the cardiac ward of the Waveney Hospital where surgery was carried out the next day. Unfortunately, despite all efforts, Mr Rooke died. It was a great shock for everyone who had met him that week and caused great sadness among the Festival members.

The Festival continued to operate as usual in the following 2 years, but by the end of 1978, financial problems forced the Committee to seek assistance from the business community. The bill for running the Festival in 1978 had risen to £5000 and there was a shortfall of £300. An emergency appeal was made to businesses who responded well, ensuring that the Festival could remain solvent for a little longer.

The next decade was to see still more turmoil, inside and outside the Festival, but towards the latter half of the eighties, a little light would begin to dawn.

# The Eighties
## 'I dreamed a dream' Les Miserables

The town of Ballymena underwent some radical changes in the 1980s with older properties being sacrificed for the advent of the new Tower Centre which eventually opened in 1982. The optimism of seeing new buildings being constructed was tempered with the knowledge that inflation was continuing to rise, along with unemployment. There was widespread dismay at factory closures, including British Enkalon in Antrim and Michelin at Mallusk. On top of economic problems, the unrest of the Northern Ireland troubles continued relentlessly.

Jim Dowds, writing in the Ballymena Observer on 28th February 1980, reminisced about the early days of the Festival, highlighting the role of Rev Strawbridge over so many years, and recounting some anecdotes about favourite adjudicators of previous years. Mr Yacamini was a music adjudicator who had endeared himself to audiences with his ready wit. Having witnessed Tom McConnell and Jack Neave trying to deliver a Scots duet with one set of scribbled words that passed back and forwards between them, Mr Yacamini had remarked 'A Scotch song apparently sung by 2 Scotsmen'

The Festival in 1980 was rather more cheering than usual because audiences were much better than in previous years. Hopes were high going into 1981 that the good news would continue but, despite good entries in many sections, the Festival was once again losing substantial sums of money. 1982 saw even greater trouble because two of the section secretaries had to resign, leaving the committee with the unenviable task of finding replacements quickly. Replacements were found, businesses contributed once again to help the Festival, so by 1983, the Festival felt itself able to be more proactive in publicising the programme and in raising funds. The new Tower Centre allowed Festival personnel to display the programme and a stall was manned to answer queries from the public. During the Festival itself, a coffee shop and a tuck shop were set up in the Town Hall to serve competitors and audience alike. Philip and Frances Smith organised the tuck shop for many years, even taking time off work to ensure their full attention. These ventures proved to be a great success and provided a regular source of income over the coming years. In 1984, the Festival was able to put £2500 into reserves, this being a direct outcome of the fundraising drive. While the Town Hall was able to house a tuck shop, no room could be found for Verse-Speaking classes which had to be held in West Church's Simpson Hall. The split venue was not ideal, but the Public Health Department had taken up residence in the Minor hall in the Town Hall, so alternative accommodation had to be found. By now, the verse-speaking section had 970 entries, well up on the previous year, in contrast to music which saw 200 fewer entries than the previous year.

Raymond Marshall resigned as Chairman in 1986 after a remarkably long involvement in the Festival, ranging from his early appearance as a boy soprano in 1929, through to playing piano in the 1930s, singing in choirs, singing as a tenor soloist, conducting choirs, and finally, overseeing the organisation for 18 years. (A full account of his life is elsewhere in this history) Rev Strawbridge had died in 1984, George Curran succeeded him as President and Samuel Hughes took over as Chairman in 1987.

The 1987 Festival was billed by the newspapers as being the Festival that almost did not happen. This was not for financial reasons, nor because of continuing political unrest, nor because of a shortage of volunteers. The problem was the heating system in the Town Hall which was undergoing refurbishment to take account of the rundown in town gas. There was a very real fear that the system could not be fixed in time for the start of the competitions, but with 24 hours to spare, Des Allen and William Young from the Council, ensured that the technical problems could be fixed. The Council also supplied floral displays which helped to give a professional appearance to the auditorium.

Also in 1987, an announcement was made regarding the establishment of a new bursary for vocalists. The bursary was for £500, and would be used for vocal tuition. This was a much more generous bursary than had ever been awarded before, and it represented the desire of the organising committee to raise the profile of the Festival among vocal competitors and also to seek out and nurture the very best voices. The bursary was paid for by Dermott Simpson and Co and was to be used to fund a new Tenor Repertoire class. The inspiration for the new competition had come from Dr Robert Simpson, who had confided his dream of finding a new tenor. Remembering that John McCormack had first come to prominence in Dublin Feis, the hope was that the prospect of a very generous prize would attract entries from the highest calibre of singers. Kathleen Regan, who was Music Secretary at the time, made the round of music schools and colleges all over Ireland and on the mainland, encouraging the best tenors to come to Ballymena in 1988. A further motivation for coming was that Ballymena Festival was prepared to provide board and lodgings so that music students would only have to pay their own travelling expenses. Kathleen Regan recruited a number of hostesses who would be willing to feed and accommodate the singers. Dr Robert Simpson christened this enterprise 'The Wren's Nest'. The hostesses became members of an elite band, 'The Wren's Nest Hospitality Club' and for 1988, and the years that followed, their generosity was acknowledged by the Festival with an annual meal when they could meet to chat over their experiences.

In 1988, the new tenor repertoire class attracted 8 entries with names such as Peter Vitale, (now a successful theatre director, actor and musician), Fraser Simpson and Randal Barnes. The organisers decided to invest the competition with even more prestige and invited two extra adjudicators to help the Festival adjudicator judge the singers. The competition was won by Finbar Wright from Cork. Finbar Wright has gone on to a glittering international singing career as a soloist, but he was also well known as being one of the three Irish Tenors along with Ronan Tynan and Anthony Kearns. Even the Belfast Telegraph was moved to send 'Rathcol' to see what was happening. One of the early adjudicators in Ballymena, Norman Hay, had himself been the very first Rathcol.

## Reviews

# Finbar wins battle of the high C's

## MUSIC

TENORS ARE a rare commodity, but that well known pronouncement by the most famous of all Rathcol's, the late Dr Norman Hay, that "the tenor voice was a disease not very prevalent in the North of Ireland", might well be extended to include the whole of these islands nowadays.

It is all more commendable, then, when a serious attempt is made in the north to find a successor to that much admired tenor, James Johnston, still happily with us, and even more so when it is linked to a provincial Music Festival, in this case that based on the Town Hall at Ballymena.

The choice of venue is particularly apt, for I am told that Count John McCormack gave one of his farewell concerts on this platform in 1938, while it was in the same lovely auditorium that a 23-year-old baritone was told that it was time to start singing tenor. His name was James Johnston.

And so, motivated by the music-loving Simpson Family, who also donated the splendid Dermot Simpson Award valued at £500, this year's Ballymena Musical Festival initiated a Tenor Repertoire Class that attracted wide support, not only from competitors, but also from the public at the event on Saturday night. The Mayor, Alderman Spence, was present.

For this competition, the official adjudicator, John Railton, was joined by Joe McKee of the BBC and John Anderson of UTV, and the excellent accompanist was Elizabeth Bicker.

One competitor from the Cork, Peter Vitale, from Wales, and Fraser Simpson, from Glasgow.

Alas, there were no entries from Belfast, but the north was represented by Randal Barnes, from Portstewart, and Brendan McCartan, who hails from Banbridge.

The set piece was Quilter's "Fair House of Joy", each competitor being allowed free choice of operatic aria or oratorio, plus an Irish song, a surprising number choosing Donazetti's "Una Furtiva" in the opera section.

Many of the contestants were young and clearly not experienced enough to make the most of their resources, and almost all showed signs of some strain at times. But the degree of involvement was heartwarming, and all acquitted themselves with much credit.

The adjudicators were unanimous in their decision, and in the end, it was experience that told, with Finbar Wright (30) proving a deserved winner, his "Trottin'" to the Fair" in particular being a real joy.

Among the remaining promising talent, two 23-year-olds deserve mention: Fraser Simpson, a fine stylist, was too slow in his "Messiah" air (but excellent in the recitative) and is worth watching; while Peter Vitale, an American from Florida on a year's Rotary Bursary to Wales, had, in my opinion, the finest natural voice. A lovely lyric but largely unschooled tenor, nerves put paid to his ability to span phrases successfully.

However, a most reward-

Rathcol gives his opinion on the new tenor repertoire class in Ballymena

Winner of the Dermott Simpson Award for Tenor Repertoire at Ballymena Music Festival was Finbar Wright from Ovens, Cork (2nd right) seen receiving the £500 award from head adjudicator Mr. John Railton. Included are accompanist Mrs. Elizabeth Bicker, and with adjudicators Mr. Joe McKee and Mr. John Anderson.

Competitors in the Dermott Simpson Tenor Repertoire Award — John Duffy (Dublin), Randall Barnes (Portstewart), winner Finbar Wright, Brendan McCartan (Banbridge), Peter Vitale (Wales), Tom Cregan (Dublin), and Fraser Simpson (Glasgow).

The new tenor repertoire class received extensive press coverage

The new Tenor Repertoire class had been very successful and other businesses now saw the advantage of sponsoring similar bursaries. Gallaher Ltd continued to support a number of small bursaries in all the disciplines but larger bursaries were funded by McKeown and Co for a Contralto voice competition with Stevenson Quarries giving a bursary for the overall winner between 7 classes. The Northern Bank also offered to fund an award for Best Instrumentalist to begin in 1990.

The Festival had suddenly become more exciting.

# The Nineties
## 'What's in a name?' Shakespeare

There was a definite sense of optimism going into the 1990s. Festival organisers had succeeded in raising morale by raising the prestige attached to competing in Ballymena Festival. Dr Robert Simpson, in his capacity as Publicity Secretary declared, *'Ballymena is the foremost country town musical festival in Northern Ireland and possibly the most exciting in the UK because no other event offers the same awards.'*

By 1990, the Festival was able to announce the Simpson Award, the Stevenson Award, the Northern Bank award for Young Musician in string, piano, woodwind or brass, as well as support from Gerrow and Wallace, Magee Clothing, and William Cumming. A new competition called 'The Ulster Award' was introduced and it was open to competitors, aged 17-35 years, in any voice category, who were both resident in Northern Ireland and had voice tuition in Northern Ireland. The prize was £500. Clearly, the organisers, while rejoicing that so many vocalists from further afield were taking part in the Simpson and Stevenson award competitions, wanted to encourage and nurture home-grown and trained talent.

James Kirkwood, the adjudicator, declared that he was astonished at the change in the music competitions since he had last visited in 1975. He said that people in England were talking about Ballymena and wondering if it could be real. *'I believe your Festival is at a stage where you must go forward.'* He urged organisers to focus on musical education to build upon what had already been achieved.

Regina Hanley, an Irish singer studying in Manchester, won the Stevenson Award. Her abilities led her to have a career in opera, later going on to become a founder member of The Celtic Divas.

In 1991, the town of Ballymena found itself with a new shopping centre with the opening of the Fairhill Centre. For many, Saturday mornings at the old Fairhill Market had epitomised Ballymena, with the stallholders promising bargains and the shoppers keen to get the best items for the best price. However, times had moved on and the geography of the town continued to change, often despite vociferous opposition from the people of the town. The Waveney Hospital, founded in 1915, was designated to be closed in favour of the new Antrim Area Hospital which was to be constructed. Many people were aghast that the town was going to be without a hospital, and campaigns were fought, unsuccessfully, to have acute services retained in Ballymena, at least until the A26, the main road between Antrim and Ballymena, could be made dual-carriageway the whole way.

At least the Festival could offer some stability and some cause for optimism. The number of large bursaries continued to rise with awards for Irish choirs, joining the already established competitions. However, the Festival was not just a musical festival, and the other disciplines of traditional dancing and Speech and Drama continued to be very popular. In 1991, a young Alison Ford, a pupil of the legendary Speech and Drama teacher, Mae McCartney, was pictured with the prizes she had won. Alison had been coming to the Festival since she was 4 years old and went on to make a career in acting, under her professional name of Alexandra Ford.

The Festival also took to heart the urgings of James Kirkwood to focus on musical education and helped to arrange a series of Masterclasses, given by one of the vocal adjudicators, Dr Heather Harper. This took place in Ballymena Academy in conjunction with the music department. The famed soprano taught on the Friday and Saturday afternoons before the Gala Evening, the grand finale of the vocal classes.

Ballymena Festival or Feis, underwent some rebranding in 1991, its 75th anniversary year, with a new logo and a new name first appearing on the syllabus and programme for 1992. Ballymena Musical Festival Association now changed its name to Ballymena Festival of Music, Speech and Dance. Adrian Hall, Head of Art and Design at Ballee Community High School, was responsible for the design of the new logo. The previous logo had featured the Seven Towers of Ballymena, the new logo gave a pictorial representation of the disciplines involved in the Festival. The logo has stood the test of time, still being used today almost 25 years later.

In 1992, the Festival received further financial support when the Association for Business Sponsorship matched the £3000 pledged for

Adrian Hall's redesigned logo for Ballymena Festival

bursaries. The Association was happy to pledge the money because it said that *'the Festival supports the social life, the educational potential and the achievements of the young people in the area.'*

In 1993, the papers featured the courage of Geraldine Donnelly, a traditional dance teacher, who had been battling cancer. Despite her problems, she had worked hard to ensure that her pupils achieved great success in the dancing competitions. Indeed, they had won so many classes that she had been given the award for the most successful teacher that year. Sadly, Geraldine was to succumb to her illness, but her name and work ethic lives on in the dancing school she founded. This was also the year that Sandy Spence ended his run as Mayor of Ballymena. He had been mayor since 1978, the longest serving Mayor of Ballymena, and had been a great friend to the Traditional music section, donating a cup to the best young tin whistle player. He had regularly attended the traditional music day which now took place on a Saturday at the beginning of February before the commencement of instrumental music classes. After many years of late Friday night sessions, the decision had been taken to stage the competition on a Saturday. Unlike all the other sections, Traditional music was unique in allowing people to enter on the day of the competition. It meant that no programme could be arranged until everyone had registered and chosen which classes to enter. There was a certain spontaneity in this method but all changed in 2013 with the decision to only allow online entry.

Aileen Logan with some of her many trophies for fiddling

In 1994, after the death of George Curran, Nancy Clarke became President of the Festival. The organisers started to hold a pre-Festival sponsors' evening where officials of the Festival would meet with the benefactors and receive cheques. This enabled the Festival to thank the contributors and also publicise the upcoming competitions. In this year, sponsors included Montgomerys, Dale Farm, Adair Arms Hotel, Gerrow and Wallace, Cameron's and the Association for Business Sponsorship.

Adjudicators continued to be impressed with the standard of the work they were shown and also with the warmth of the welcome they had received. Mrs Alison Walker-Moorcroft adjudicated in instrumental music and said *'I have had the privilege of spotting some real stars in the making; some performances have been a revelation. Standards here are just amazing.'* Sally Noble, the Speech and Drama adjudicator said, *'The local hospitality has been marvellous'* and they both agreed *'Everyone looks after everyone else.'*

So far, the Festival had congratulated itself on attracting singers from all over Ireland and Britain, but there was to be a competitor from further afield in 1995. This had arisen from a chance meeting on a aeroplane journey when Elizabeth Black, from Ballymena, fell into conversation with the young lady seated next to her. It transpired that the young lady, Eva Erika Trudso, was a Danish singing student. Elizabeth Black seized the opportunity to invite her to sing at Ballymena, posting the entry forms to Copenhagen along with an offer to accommodate her if she chose to come. Eva, a student of Kim Borg, a well-known professor of music at the Conservatoire in Copenhagen, accepted the invitation and sang with great success in Ballymena. She won the Raymond S Marshall challenge cup and medal for Grand Opera solo along with the Hubert McCullough award for most promising adult vocal solo. Eva Trudso pronounced herself to be amazed at the warmth of the welcome she had received from everyone. She also explained,

*'Young people in Denmark don't have many opportunities like this to perform and compete. I think your festival is wonderful.'*

In 1996, the Festival had a further rebranding when, as a result of significant sponsorship, the Festival advertised itself as 'Ulster Maid Ballymena Festival of Music, Speech and Dance'. The Festival saw some wonderful performances and much tribute was paid to a young singer, Carolyn Dobbin, from Carrickfergus. She was the eventual winner of the Stevenson award, but it was her performance in the Irish Song section of the Female voice repertoire that seemed to cast a spell over audience and adjudicator alike. She sang 'She moved through the fair' so beautifully that the adjudicator awarded her 90 marks, remarking that,

'The divine was not in the thunder, was not in the earthquake. It was in the still, small voice.'

Carolyn Dobbin was nominated by Ballymena Festival to take part in a national 'Festival of Festivals' that was being run in July that year by the British Federation of Festivals in order to celebrate their 75th anniversary. She was one of only two people to win a gold medal in the vocal music section of that prestigious competition. Ballymena Festival nominee for Speech and Drama, Christopher Logan, was equally successful in winning a gold medal. The dance nominee for the Festival of Festivals was Ian Mackay. Carolyn Dobbin was initially set to have a career as an art teacher, but she enjoyed such success with her singing that she eventually became a professional singer.

Back in Ballymena, the success of the Festival was even talked about in the Council Chamber. James Currie, at that time deputy mayor, pointed out that the vocal music adjudicator, T Gwynne Jones, had described Ballymena as being 'one of the best run competitions he had ever been to and one of the best Festivals in Northern Ireland.' James Currie also went on to praise and thank the volunteers behind the scenes who worked so hard and who had succeeded in restoring the Festival to its former glory.

Ballymena Festival had grown accustomed to hosting singers from all over the country, but it caused a bit of a stir in 1997 when an 11 year-old boy from London, Dominic Yeu, entered piano competitions. In 1998, the biggest story in Ballymena was the proposed new town hall which would, of course, have major implications for the Festival. There would be no possibility of the Festival taking place in its usual home while the renovations and extensions were under way. The members of the Borough Council was also much exercised by the problems of car-parking in the town. Some things never change.

With the approach of the Millennium, the world grew anxious at the possibility of 'The Millennium Bug' causing computer meltdown. The Festival had no such worries because it had not yet ventured into the world of the internet. That was eventually to change, enabling Ballymena Festival to have a website and the possibility for section secretaries to reduce drastically the amount of time needed to cope with the paperwork.

The Festival was about to join the twenty-first century.

# The Twenty-First Century
## 'The Show must go on'

The fears that the Millennium Bug would paralyse the world came to nothing and, in fact, it was a very different sort of bug that caused misery over the festive period of 1999-2000. There was a very severe 'flu outbreak all over the country, putting pressure on the Health Service's ability to cope with a marked increase of admissions coupled with staff shortages. Things were on a more even keel by the time 'Ballymena Millennium Festival' came around and all ran smoothly. By 2001, the Festival had a new President, with Mrs Dorothy Simpson (nee Strawbridge) taking up the position. The chairman, Samuel Hughes, was ill during the Festival and was unable to be present. Ballymena Borough Council became the main sponsors of the Festival in 2001 and there was much speculation and anticipation about the proposed new Town Hall complex. The new Town Hall was to include a museum and the Heritage Lottery Fund granted £4.44 million towards its construction. The Festival was just over when the Foot and Mouth crisis began; had this occurred earlier it could have had a huge impact on the numbers of people prepared to travel in from the countryside. As it was, the Festival knew that changes were on the way, and indeed, this was the last year for the activities to take place in the Town Hall. For the next 6 years, Ballymena Festival was on the move.

In 2002, the Festival took place in Hotel One, the name at that time for Leighinmohr House Hotel. There is no doubt that there was less room than in the Town Hall, but the organisers were determined to make the best of the situation. Throughout the time of the exile from the Town Hall, some choir classes took place in Ballymena North Community Centre, the hotel being unable to accommodate the very large numbers involved.

The change of venue from the Town Hall had certainly not discouraged the usual large entries. In Speech and Drama, a record 20 groups took part in choral verse speaking. There was a further change of venue in 2007 when the Adair Arms hosted the Festival. The Adair Arms has been the traditional hotel used to accommodate adjudicators over the years and many have spoken highly of the hospitality they have enjoyed. With events happening so close to their accommodation, adjudicators had minimal travelling time to eat into their busy schedule, although it must have felt at times like living above the shop.

Stanley Hughes took over as chairman in 2003, after the sad death of Samuel Hughes. Irene Cumming became President of the Festival in 2004 and together, Stanley Hughes and Irene Cumming have remained in their respective positions. By 2004, details were beginning to emerge about the Town Hall complex, with many councillors dismayed that the seating capacity of the auditorium was going to be greatly reduced. Before refurbishment, the hall could seat 600, this was now to be reduced to 400. The architects explained that they were required to follow new health and safety guidelines and that it was simply impossible to seat as many people as before. This was potentially a problem for the Festival, and indeed, it has proved to be difficult to seat everyone on days when there are large numbers of choirs coupled with parents who wish to enjoy the performance.

In 2005, Dr Andrew Hudson became Instrumental Secretary. Besides his work in making sure that instrumental music classes ran smoothly, he was also keen to allow festival administration to benefit from the use of computers. This was accomplished by degrees and the initial task was to create a database of class definitions that could be used to make the production of the syllabus and the programme less complicated. (A fuller explanation of the computer revolution in Ballymena Festival is given elsewhere in this history).

In February 2008, The Braid, the newly named Town Hall, opened its doors to let the people of the town see its transformation.

The Braid Town Hall, Museum and
Arts Centre opened its doors in 2008
*Image courtesy of Mid and East Antrim Museum at the Braid*

The architects had married old and new together, creating a dramatic building right in the heart of the town. Those who flocked to the Open Day pronounced themselves very impressed with the building and the facilities it offered. The Deputy Mayor, P J McAvoy, spoke of the Council's pride in the new centre and said how delighted he was to be able to welcome Ballymena Festival 'home'. The Council members were determined to mark this special year and to celebrate the opening of The Braid, it was announced that Ballymena Borough Council would fund 3 special awards of £500 to the winners of certain classes in choir, orchestra and choral speaking. In the Traditional music section, thanks to the generosity of the Council, 3 competitors were awarded scholarships by the Braid Arts Centre to attend an International Arts Festival in Morehead, Kentucky, the sister town to Ballymena in the United States. The lucky recipients were Siobhan Molloy, Joe Murray and Austin Donnelly and they were given the responsibility of representing Ballymena Borough Council in Morehead.

Now that the Festival was settled back into its normal abode, the organisers continued to try to attract entries from as wide an area as possible. In 2010, entries came for the vocal section from all over Northern Ireland, from London, Dublin, and the Isle of Man. Entries were so large that the section secretary had to organise 3 extra days of competitions and add 2 extra adjudicators.

The Festival was delighted to present a Lifetime Achievement award in 2011, not to a committee member, but to a gentleman who had been competing in the traditional music section for 40 years. Jim Kyle, 80, from Lisburn, first entered the Violin Sacred Solo competition in 1971 and he had been returning, usually with great success, ever since. It certainly proved that Ballymena Festival could cater for all ages.

Traditional musicians from Ballymena
and Norway meet in Ballymena Library

There was an international flavour to the Traditional section that year with Ballymena playing host to some Norwegian visitors. Two special events were organised, with Ballymena Library being the venue for an evening of traditional song and story-telling from Co Antrim and Telemark, Norway. Two gentlemen from Norway, Arnfinn Staurheim and Alf Gjessing, joined forces with Colin McAllister, the Traditional Music adjudicator that year, to entertain the audience with stories and songs. A further occasion for international cooperation came with a Traditional Singing workshop, held in Houston's Mill in Broughshane. The audience on both occasions learned about the remarkable similarities between Norwegian and Ulster traditions.

Jim Kyle receives gifts to mark his contribution to the Festival over 40 years
*(reproduced by permission of Ballymena Times)*

In the summer of 2013, an Extraordinary Committee Meeting was called to hear a submission from a group who wished to begin a Modern Dance section. The delegation explained that their children attended modern dance classes in Ballymena and that they had been taking part in competitions in various towns in Northern Ireland. Their hope was that the Festival would permit them to stage modern dance competitions in Ballymena, revealing that audience figures were generally high for modern dance competitions and that there was a definite potential for attracting visitors to the town. The committee members, in conjunction with Arts and Development Officer, Rosalind Lowry, agreed in principle that the first year's competitions would take place in 2014 under the umbrella of the Arts Festival and that Modern Dance would be fully assimilated into Ballymena Festival by 2015. The first Modern Dance competitions took place in March 2014 and they were very successful; they were well organised and provided a colourful new discipline within the Festival. Over the years, the Festival had always been prepared to evolve and adapt, and the decision to admit Modern Dance into the Festival was entirely in keeping with tradition. A further evidence of the Festival's willingness to embrace change had come in 2010 with the provision of a Festival website. The aim was to have a one-stop shop which could receive and provide information to committee and public alike.

In 2014, Irene Cumming, President of the Festival, was honoured with a British Empire Medal for her services to the community and to the Festival for over 40 years and she was congratulated by the Festival committee who told the press,

> 'This is taken not only to be in recognition of Irene's involvement in promoting the Arts in the Ballymena area, but also the high esteem in which the Festival is held in the Ballymena area and throughout N Ireland. Irene, who last year received the Federation's Award for long service, is a very 'hands on' President. This is evidenced during the annual Festival through her attendance at all the various competitions but especially by her personal involvement in the Speech and Drama Section.'

Typically, Irene Cumming declared that she accepted the honour on behalf of all those who had worked alongside her in the Festival.

In 2015, the outgoing Ballymena Borough Council invited the public to nominate organisations and individuals whose contribution to the community merited recognition. Ballymena Festival of Music, Speech and Dance was not only nominated but received an Exceptional Recognition Award, to emphasise the esteem in which it was held for its encouragement of talent throughout the community.

Preparations for the celebration of the centenary in 2016 had begun a number of years before but they gathered pace in 2015. It was agreed to hold a special concert in The Braid on 13th February 2016. This would serve to launch the celebrations and to highlight the centenary to the public. The decision was also taken to issue special prize-winners badges, to be finished in gold, silver and bronze effect, and to be presented only in the centenary year. These were to be based on original badges or medals issued by the Ballymena Musical Festival Association.

The Festival applied to the Heritage Lottery Fund for financial aid to mark the centenary properly. This was granted through the 'Sharing Heritage' programme, enabling the Festival organisers to go the extra mile in celebrating the centenary. The money from the HLF enabled the writing and publication of this commemorative book on the history of the Festival. It also funded the printing of special certificates of participation to be awarded to everyone performing in the Centenary Festival 2016. Specially commissioned copies of the original gold medal awarded in 1916 are to be given as mementoes to members, volunteers and sponsors as a token of appreciation for their contribution over the years. Plans for centenary celebrations also included mounting an exhibition to illustrate the history of the Festival, again to be funded by Heritage Lottery fund.

The purpose in all this activity was never to draw attention to one person, or to one section. Ballymena Festival has continued to flourish because of the people involved over the years, people who have come from all sections of the community, from all classes and, increasingly, from many nationalities. There have been triumphs, with breath-taking performances over the years. There have been difficulties, with circumstances beyond anyone's control conspiring to dishearten and demoralise. There have been tears, of nervousness and disappointment, of sorrow and of joy. There has been laughter, much laughter, and the development of bonds of friendship and comradeship among organisers and competitors alike. Successive generations of organisers have devoted long hours of work for no monetary gain whatsoever. Generations of performers have come to the Feis to show what they can do and to receive advice on how they can do better. Somehow, this has lasted for 100 years with no sign of the story being over.

The Show still goes on.

Dorothy Strawbridge, centre, pictured with Sammy
Houston after her success in a piano competition.

Dorothy Strawbridge pictured outside the
Town Hall. Much later, as Dorothy Simpson,
she became President of the Festival.

Folk-dancers, including a young Raymond Marshall, in the 1930s.

Mary Barr recruited local children to sing in her
choirs, these were some members in the 1940s.

Children from Lisnamurrican Primary School show the trophies won at Ballymena Festival. James Nesbitt is pictured front row, third from left.

Newbridge CCE were judged winners of Traditional Junior Instrumental
Group 2012, reproduced by permission of Ballymena Times.

Ballymena Chamber Orchestra on stage in Ballymena Festival in 2013.

Cullybackey WI choir taking part in the Festival in 1992.

Sadie Bell founded the Seven Towers School of Dance. She is shown
here in the centre of the picture, surrounded by well-wishers.

Raymond Marshall treasured the card given
on his retirement by members of the Festival.

Emma Martin and Sophie McKeegan from the Royal Tara School
of Dancing, reproduced by permission of Ballymena Times.

Suzanna Gorecka taking part in Ballymena
Festival's traditional dance section.

Katie, Hillie and Abby from Ballymena Dance
Academy taking part in Modern Dance.

Attendance Dance Company pictured at the Festival in 2014.

Stephen Rankin receives his Beggs and Partners Young Instrumentalist
award in 2011, reproduced by permission of Ballymena Times.

Helen Aiken receiving the Stevenson award in 2011. From left, Marilynne Davies, adjudicator, Irene Cumming, President, Helen Aiken, Stanley Hughes, Chairman.

School and junior prize-winners, together with their teachers,
smile for the camera after the Gala night in 2014.

P J McAvoy surrounded by officials and volunteers before the Stewards Breakfast in
the Adair Arms Hotel, reproduced by permission of Ballymena Times.

Officials and volunteers gather for the pre-launch festival breakfast in 2014.

The Mayor, Audrey Wales, attended the launch breakfast in 2014.

Irene Cumming, President, presents Jack and Kathleen Regan
with gifts to mark their more than 40 year involvement with
the Festival, reproduced by permission of Ballymena Times.

# Section 2

## The Hall of Fame

O ver its hundred year history, thousands of people have been involved in Ballymena Festival, whether as performers or organisers or teachers. In this section, the intention is to highlight a number who have either made a significant contribution to Ballymena Festival or who themselves have been affected by their participation. The chosen personalities are placed here in approximate chronological order.

# 'The Visionary'
## Mrs Dinsmore

Mrs Dinsmore was born Mary Elizabeth Brown Irwin on 14 July 1864 in Bandon, County Cork. Her father, Rev Dr William Irwin, a native of Co Londonderry, was the Presbyterian minister in Bandon. Mary was the middle daughter of 9 children. It was clearly a well-educated family since 3 of her brothers became Presbyterian ministers and Mary herself, along with two other sisters, worked as a teacher. Sometime between 1871 and 1901, the family moved back north and lived in the Coleraine area.

In 1909 Mary, now aged 45, married the widowed John Dinsmore JP of Kells and came to live in Crebilly Castle. Her husband was the proprietor of J Dinsmore and Son, Woollen Manufacturers, Kells. His public service had included being a Poor Law guardian for many years and he had been an Antrim County Councillor until 1905. His political views were rather unusual in that, as a Protestant, he was in favour of Home Rule for Ireland. It is quite likely that Mary, having been born and brought up in Co Cork, would have had a more accepting attitude than most of her friends and neighbours towards the idea of Home Rule and she may have had some influence on her husband's thinking. Mrs Dinsmore was described as being a famed musician and linguist. With her background in teaching, it is not difficult to see how she would have decided that a musical festival was just the thing that Ballymena needed and deserved. Her intention was to reach the young so that they would be the musicians of the future. Contemporary accounts tell of a woman who was determined and resolute, passionate and able to persuade even those who had doubts and fears.

She was heavily involved in the hard work of getting the Festival under way and was fully committed to its success. It must have come as a huge shock to the association when, in 1919, with the Festival only in its infancy, she and her husband moved from the district. Mrs Brabazon, her fellow secretary, also left Ballymena that year. Nevertheless, the Festival, having been established on a firm foundation, continued to flourish. Mrs Dinsmore made an effort to visit the Festival year after year and never failed to send a telegram of good wishes if she was unable to attend in person. She died in 1935 in Newhaven, Sussex.

Mary Dinsmore's name is perpetuated in trophies that are still awarded today to Primary School choirs competing in Ballymena Festival. The musical education infrastructure that exists today would have been the stuff of dreams for Mrs Dinsmore, yet her commitment to the establishment of a musical festival in Ballymena was one decisive step along the path to making her dreams a reality.

# 'The Secretary'
## Mrs Wier

Mrs Ruth Wier was one of those people who attended the initial meeting in June 1915 when Mrs Dinsmore proposed the organisation of a music festival in Ballymena. At that stage she was a young wife and mother who was already committed to war work with SSAFA (Soldiers, Sailors, Airmen and Families Association) along with her work as an official War Pensions visitor. Nevertheless, being a lover of music, she decided to become involved with the fledgling organisation and so began many years of loyal service to Ballymena Musical Festival Association. Mrs Wier had come to Ballymena as a bride in 1909. Born and raised in Lancashire, the daughter of a builder's merchant, she married William Wier, a journalist from Ballymena, whose father was the editor of the Ballymena Observer. Together, they had four children, a son and three daughters.

In 1919, just as the Festival was getting established, Mrs Dinsmore and Mrs Brabazon left the district, leaving the committee aghast and the post of secretary needing to be filled. Mrs Wier, along with Mrs Currie accepted the task and they set to work with Mrs Wier eventually becoming General Secretary. It soon became obvious that she was born for the role. As the Festival expanded and the work grew more onerous, Mrs Wier seemed to thrive. She was responsible for booking adjudicators, organising the syllabus, receiving entries, devising the programme and the venues required. Year after year, the newspapers reported the glowing compliments that were paid to Mrs Wier by the chairman and the adjudicators. She was clearly an efficient organiser with an eye to detail but she was also unfailingly courteous and tactful when dealing with people. In addition to her secretarial duties during the festival, Mrs Wier also provided an evening meal at home for the chairman and the adjudicators! One adjudicator spoke of her as being 'kindness itself.' Another spoke of the 'clockwork precision' of the arrangements. Mrs Wier simply loved the Festival and its success was the only reward she sought.

The Festival was suspended during the war years 1939 - 1945 but the time came in June 1945 for the committee to gather to plan for the future. Mrs Wier resigned as secretary, explaining that it was impossible for her to take up the burden once more. Unsurprisingly, it was only with the greatest reluctance that the committee accepted her resignation. She remained a committed member of the association but she was wise enough to realise her limitations. Her husband was in declining health and he died in May 1946.

Mrs Wier may not have been a native of Ballymena but the town had cause to be grateful to her for unceasing service in many areas. She was instrumental in founding Ballymena Comforts Fund, which raised money for sending parcels to local

Mrs Wier is seen outside the Town Hall in the 1930s

people serving in the 1939-45 war. She was involved at committee level in the British Legion, the Forces Help Society, and Lord Robert's Workshops. Her interest in forces' welfare during the war was entirely understandable since all her children served abroad. She served on the Ballymena and District Nursing Committee and the Cottage Hospital Committee. She was the founder president of Ballymena Business and Professional Women's Club and in 1943 was a founder member of CEMA - a forerunner to the Arts Council.

She was able to indulge her love of music with her membership of the Philharmonic Society and was president of the Linenhall choir which over many years played a huge role in the cultural life of the town.

Mrs Wier was awarded an MBE in June 1962 for her public service. In 1964, the mayor, having been presented with insignia donated by Mrs Wier's Business and Professional Women's Club, said that he did not know what Ballymena would have done without Mrs Wier and indeed he thought of her as a kind of 'Winston Churchill of Ballymena'.

Mrs Wier eventually moved to Bristol to stay with one of her daughters. She died there in December 1979.

Ruth Wier was an extraordinarily gifted organiser and a woman who was prepared to work hard without any financial reward. It is interesting to note that she was involved in areas that tried to make life better for people, whether through welfare provision for the vulnerable or the encouragement of the practice and appreciation of the arts. It is only right that her contribution to the development of the Festival is remembered and celebrated.

# 'The Teacher'
## Miss Bowen-Evans

Miss Edith Bowen-Evans arrived in Ballymena in 1910 to take up a part-time appointment as music mistress in the newly founded Cambridge House School for girls. She was born in LLanasa, Flintshire, Wales, in 1880, youngest daughter of Thomas and Jemima Evans. Her father was a lead miner. When she came to Ballymena she initially lived as a boarder in a house in Lawn View Place. In addition to her duties in school, Miss Bowen-Evans gave private piano and voice lessons in her studio in Linenhall Street. She stayed at Cambridge House until 1919 where she obviously made a strong impression on the girls.

> 'A real Tartar. She often wore a velvet jacket like a smoking jacket, with a black skirt and stockings. She had short hair like a man and she wore a man's hat. Everyone was terrified of her. She once fell off the platform on the Town Hall while conducting the choir.'

(The speaker is unknown, but was quoted in Cambridge House 75 year commemorative history)

Miss Bowen-Evans may have been terrifying but she was an excellent teacher. She excelled in voice training with both choirs and individual pupils flourishing under her tutelage. She founded a number of choirs, most notably the Linenhall choirs which became well-known in Ballymena and far beyond. The Linenhall Mixed Voice choir featured in a BBC radio programme on 17th June 1939 'The Country comes to town.' It also contributed to programmes for the Forces during the war. Some of her pupils who achieved great success in their singing career included Raymond Marshall and Mary Murray (later Mrs Barr). She advertised in the local papers her ability to teach 'Pianoforte playing, rudiments and harmony, solo singing, junior choirs and percussion band'. She had moved from her first studio in Linenhall Street to a studio in Castle Street.

Miss Bowen-Evans was an enthusiastic supporter of Ballymena Musical Festival and for many years she entered individual pupils for

Miss Bowen-Evans advertised regularly in the local papers

competition and also choirs, sometimes conducting several choirs in the various competitions. Her standards were high, her discipline unyielding but she and her singers achieved her aim of making wonderful music for all to enjoy.

She was forced to retire through ill-health in 1946 and moved back to her home village of Llanasa. Her pupils and colleagues organised a retirement dinner for her and presented her with a sizeable amount of money to show their appreciation. The local newspapers reported that

*'Miss Bowen-Evans was overwhelmed by kindness and the nice things said about her. She appreciated the friendliness and generosity of Ballymena for over 30 years. 'Don't throw up your music. It is culture, it opens up a passage of the mind.' She had enjoyed training the choirs tremendously and added that she appreciated all they had done for her and all they stood from her.' Her last sentence was greeted with laughter.*

Miss Bowen-Evans did not regain her health but died 2 February 1947. Her obituary in a local Ballymena newspaper paid tribute to her musical influence in the town.

*'When one recalls the number of local artists who during the last quarter of a century or so graced concert platforms or took part in competitions at Ballymena Musical Festival, it is amazing just how many of these were her pupils. Nothing but the best in music satisfied her, that is why she was so painstaking and such a disciplinarian. She knew that half-hearted efforts would never get pupils or choirs anywhere.'*

In March 1947, Rev Strawbridge, chairman of the Festival Association spoke of her fondly at the beginning of the next Festival after her death.

*'There is one other thing I must say. I would be remiss in my*

*duty if I did not make reference at the beginning of this week to the great loss our Association has sustained, since last Festival, through the death of Miss E Bowen-Evans. She was a professional Teacher of Music and, of course, was primarily concerned with her own work - a work for which she simply lived. Perhaps there was no one person who did so much, on the musical side, to achieve the objects we have in view and to raise the standard of our annual Festival to the high position which it has attained.'*

A cup in memory of Miss Bowen-Evans was presented to the Festival in 1948 to be awarded to adult choirs. After her death, the Linenhall choirs were conducted by Goodlett Leetch initially, and then by Raymond Marshall.

Miss Bowen-Evans played a pivotal role in the development of music in Ballymena generally and in the Festival in particular. Her methods may have been draconian, especially by today's standards, but her love of music was the driving force of her life.

# 'The Chairman'
## Rev Robert Strawbridge

Rev Robert Strawbridge was Ballymena Festival's longest serving chairman to date.. He became chairman in 1933 and remained in post for 35 years, a remarkable achievement by any standards, and a record that is unlikely ever to be surpassed.

Like so many other pivotal characters in Ballymena Festival, Rev Strawbridge did not come from the town. He was born in 1892 to a farming family in Ballydermot, Co Londonderry and was one of 10 children. Music always played an important part in his life and as a student he was a member of Derry Glee and Madrigal Society. Once his studies were complete, Rev Strawbridge enlisted in the army to help with the war effort and began Officer training. Upon demobilisation, he served as minister in Banbridge Road Presbyterian Church in Dromore for a year until, in 1920, he was ordained to the ministry in 1st Broughshane Presbyterian Church. His marriage to his wife Anne McMullan came not long after and together they settled into life in Broughshane. They had four daughters, Moira, Kathleen, Dorothy and Patricia, all of whom became accustomed to sharing their father and mother with the annual Ballymena Festival. Patricia (now Paddy Wallace) recalls having to come in to the Town Hall to do her homework after school because her mother and father were both occupied with supervising competitions. The girls also took part in various classes, including piano, singing and verse-speaking.

Rev Strawbridge was an enthusiastic and meticulous chairman. His military training may have had an influence on his ability to deal as efficiently as possible with getting choirs on and off stage. He loved children and saw the Festival as being a wonderful way of exposing them to the appreciation of good music, dance and verse-speaking. It was clear that he felt the frustration of dwindling audiences, but he was convinced of the value of carrying on for the sake of the children who were taking part in the Festival.

In life outside the Festival, Rev Strawbridge proved himself to be a diligent and hard-working minister to his congregation. When he arrived in Broughshane, there was no organ and only psalms were sung. The church building was also in need of extension and repair and he succeeded in steering the church through a period of change with great diplomacy. He was also able to indulge his love of music with his membership of Ballymena Philharmonic Society, also singing with the Linenhall Mixed Voice choir.

When Rev Strawbridge retired from active ministry in Broughshane in 1963, his congregation paid him many compliments and he agreed to be Senior Minister. The church recognised his gifts as a preacher, teacher and friend and the Clerk of Session said,

Rev Strawbridge in his early days as Chairman of Ballymena Festival

*'He has been the first friend we want to have with us in times of either joy or sorrow.'*

The Committee of Ballymena Festival felt equally privileged to have had Rev Strawbridge as their chairman for so many years. He announced his retirement in 1968, after 35 years of service to the Festival, declaring that he had never expected to be in the position for as long. He accepted the Committee's invitation to become the first President of the Festival. He held that position until his death in 1984.

Mrs Wier presented a gift to Rev Strawbridge to mark his 25 years as Chairman

Rev Strawbridge had steered the Festival through the highs of the years when the Town Hall was packed out, through the lows of the years when dwindling audiences made the committee question the wisdom of carrying on and through the distractions of wireless and television and, as he put it, 'manias of all sorts'. His commitment to the Festival was steadfast and an example to all.

The epitaph on his gravestone is simple. 'He was a good man'.

# 'The Tenor who thought he was a baritone'
## James Johnston

James Johnston, or Jim as he was known, was the son of a butcher from Sandy Row in Belfast. He participated very successfully in many festivals and singing competitions but when he entered the baritone class in Ballymena Festival in 1925, the adjudicator, E T Davies, astonished him by saying that he couldn't award the first prize to him because he wasn't a baritone, he was a tenor!

> '..where the range of the song suited, it gave the adjudicators great pleasure...one was conscious of the tenor timbre of the tone'

> '..at present he was singing baritone but he (the adjudicator E T Davies) was perfectly convinced he would make not a good local tenor but a great tenor.'

The adjudicator further went on to appeal for someone in the audience to fund musical studies abroad so that the young man's potential could be realised.

James Johnston was disappointed at the adjudicator's decision, not least because he felt it would have an adverse bearing on any future baritone competitions he might enter. Soon afterwards, a gentleman who had been in the audience at Ballymena Festival came to James Johnston's father's butcher's shop where the young man also worked, and offered to pay for him to study abroad with a view to becoming an operatic tenor. James Johnston's father, a strict Methodist, threw him out of the shop declaring that the stage was no place for his son. James continued to sing as an amateur, receiving local vocal tuition, but by now he had accepted the adjudicator's advice that he was a tenor. He was a member of the Cedar Quartet and he also sang in oratorio performances throughout Ireland. In the 1930s he became the paid tenor in St Anne's Cathedral. His father's opposition to the stage meant that he felt that he could not study at a formal level in keeping with his potential. James Johnston did, however, eventually become involved with Dublin Operatic Society and sang with them from 1940-1945. James Johnston was still singing as an amateur because he had followed in his father's footsteps and now owned a number of butcher's shops in Belfast.

In 1945, Tyrone Guthrie, by then in charge of Sadler's Wells Opera Company, and coincidentally a former adjudicator in Verse-Speaking at Ballymena Festival, approached James Johnston to consider singing in London with Sadler's Wells. James resisted at first, declaring that he had only amateur experience. Possibly in an attempt to put Guthrie off, James Johnston insisted on having a leading role before he would come across. Guthrie agreed, so James Johnston made the move to London. His family still disapproved of his singing career, but the London audiences loved him. Eventually, he became principal tenor in Covent Garden and sang with many great artists including Joan Sutherland, Elizabeth Schwarzkopf and Maria Callas. He had a hugely successful operatic career, being a favourite of critics and audiences alike. He retained his Belfast accent and his no-nonsense approach to life, treating all those he met, whether rich or poor, as equals.

James Johnston, popularly known as 'The Singing Butcher'
*Image courtesy of the Belfast Telegraph*

Dr Havelock Nelson, OBE wrote in appreciation of him,

> *'All of us who worked with Jimmy can never forget the vitality and beauty of his voice, his natural artistry and the incredible*

*clarity of his words. Had he lived in the period of the 1970s or 1980s he would have been snowed under with recording contracts. As it is, the few recordings that he made are treasured by his many admirers as mementoes of a truly great voice and musical personality.'*

James Johnston sang in London for the last time in 1958, having declared that he would retire while still at the top, and then returned to Belfast where he worked as a butcher, content to sing his arias to the housewives of Sandy Row.

Perhaps it is overstating the case to declare that Ballymena Festival had a pivotal role to play in the career of James Johnston. What is certain, is that what the adjudicator, E T Davies, said to him caused a change in direction in his singing career. Mr Davies lived to see James Johnston's success as a tenor, and it must be supposed that it gave him a great deal of satisfaction to see that James Johnston was most definitely a tenor, not just a good local tenor, but a great tenor.

# 'The Singer'
## Mary Barr

Mary Barr was born Mary Murray and from an early age her great passion was music, and singing in particular. She was a pupil of Miss Bowen-Evans and her vocal prowess was well known at Ballymena Festival being a popular winner of the Wier Silver Potato Ring and the prestigious Morton cup as well as many other trophies.

Mary Murray pictured in 1932 with
her trophies

She was small in stature but she had a very powerful and true singing voice that could fill any hall without the need for any amplification.

As well as singing herself, Mary taught piano and vocal students, also forming her own choirs whose members were recruited from her local neighbourhood of Albert Place, Fountain Place and High Street. None of her family members were allowed to escape from joining the choir either. Choir rehearsals of her Albert Chorus took place in her often overcrowded loft. She was a strict teacher, wanting the best from her pupils, but she was always very proud of them all and earned their deepest respect in return.

Mary seen with some of her choir members in 1965

Throughout her teaching career Mary was responsible for producing some exceptional talent. Harold Alexander, now deceased, went on to become a renowned and talented choirmaster who was respected throughout the province and beyond. Phoebe McDonald, née Robinson, herself a talented singer and musician, has gone on to make teaching music her career, in turn training choirs to prizewinning standard.

Mary Barr lived to a ripe old age, dying in September 2004 in her 91st year. She is remembered fondly by her family, her pupils and the members of her Albert Chorus who literally made the rafters of her loft ring.

Mary Barr with some of the trophies won by her pupils

# 'The All-Rounder'
## Raymond Marshall

Raymond Marshall was chairman of the Festival from 1968 until 1986. It must have been a daunting task to take over from the long-serving Rev Strawbridge, but Raymond Marshall was undoubtedly qualified for the role. Ballymena Festival was in his blood.

The young Raymond Marshall had first appeared at Ballymena Festival as a boy soprano back in 1929. He also played piano and entered piano classes in the 1930s while his voice matured into its full tenor glory. As a pupil of Miss Bowen-Evans, he was to receive tuition of the highest standard and eventually became a tenor soloist in great demand all over Northern Ireland. The Studio Opera Group was formed in 1950 and Raymond Marshall was a valued member and friend of its founder, Havelock Nelson. He sang as tenor soloist in all the great oratorios and sang on BBC Northern Ireland more than 50 times, appearing on programmes like 'Come into the Parlour', 'Children's Hour', 'Ulster

Raymond Marshall with the Linenhall choir in Ballymena Town Hall

Serenade' and 'Ulster Band'. Back in Ballymena he was also a member of the Linenhall choir and regularly competed with them in Ballymena Festival.

Raymond Marshall was also a skilled choirmaster; he eventually became conductor of Linenhall Ladies and Linenhall Mixed Voice Choirs, again conducting them in competition in Ballymena and in other Festivals. He took Linenhall Ladies choir to London to participate in the Festival of Britain National Ladies Choir competition. In 1965, he began to conduct the Seven Towers Male Voice Choir, taking them on tour to Canada in 1979, to Wales in 1980 and to Scotland in 1984 and 1986.

Raymond Marshall had other interests besides music; in his early days he was an active member of the Church Lads' Brigade based in St Patrick's Church and was an excellent badminton player, playing for Ulster on several occasions.

Nevertheless, music remained Raymond's greatest passion. In all his endeavours he was supported by his wife, Grace, who worked alongside him in the Festival, as Music Secretary from 1967-1980, but also in the family grocery business. They admitted that during Festival time, they saw very little of the shop, such were the demands placed upon them. Raymond became chairman at a difficult time in the history of the Festival. Financial difficulties at times threatened to overwhelm the members and the effects of political turmoil became more apparent. Despite the difficulties and frustrations, members of the press always remarked on his genial manner and his willingness to be of assistance to them. Although Raymond Marshall had experienced the Festival in the days of crowded halls and capacity audiences, he refused to give up and was prepared to accept new ways of raising money to keep the Festival afloat.

Grace Marshall died in 1983, mourned by her husband and the other members of the Festival Association. Raymond kept the notes of the tribute paid to her by George Curran on behalf of the Festival and he also kept the card, signed by all the members, which was presented to him when he retired from the Festival in 1986.

Ballymena Festival was the richer for having him so closely involved for so many years. Raymond Marshall eventually died in 2006 but his memory is perpetuated with The Raymond S Marshall Challenge Cup, presented to the winner of the Operatic Solo class.

# 'The Musician'
## Rose Murray

Rose Murray has been associated with Ballymena Festival since 1967 when she began to play piano to accompany the traditional dance classes. That first year, full of trepidation, she had to play alone but since then she has been joined by many other musicians and together they have provided the music for the jigs and reels of the colourful event. Rose's sister, Lily Agnew, was a champion Irish dancer, and the family ties with the Festival go back to the 1940s and 1950s when her uncles, James and Robbie Carmichael, played their fiddle and banjo to accompany the dancing.

Lily Agnew, with her uncles who played for traditional dancing at Ballymena

Rose began piano lessons when she was 8 and continued them until she was 20. Her teacher was Miss Wylie, Ballymoney Road, who taught classical pieces. Rose was heavily influenced by the traditional music she heard at home and picked up the traditional pieces herself. Her adaptability was also seen when she played for the Irish Ballet Group in the late 1950s and early 1960s, even playing twice at the Edinburgh Festival. She also played for a Scottish dancing class in Ballymena where her talent stood out.

Rose first became involved as a pianist for Ballymena Festival when her name was put forward by Mrs Jean Tennant, a well-known dance teacher. However, her memories of the Festival go back much further, because she can recall being taken to the Town Hall to watch her sister, Lily Agnew, triumphing in the Senior Championship. 'I recall seeing people queuing down Bridge Street on the Saturday night to get in to watch the Senior Teams and Solo Dancers at the Festival.'

Rose recalls that in the early days, the dancing section was organised by a dedicated committee of people who ran the dancing festival with great efficiency and dignity. In many cases, they had little personal knowledge of Irish dancing but were prepared to do their best to ensure that the section ran smoothly.

She has had her fair share of embarrassing moments. She recounts, 'When the dancing took place on the large floor of the Town Hall and the musicians sat on the same level, I remember my sister bringing my small daughter, about 18 months old at the time, to see the dancers and hear her mummy playing. To my horror, I watched her run onto the middle of the floor and start running around right in front of a competitor. I was so embarrassed that I pretended I didn't know the child. I cringed when it was announced that 'People must keep their children under control!''

A musician's view of dancing before the refurbishment of the Town Hall

Rose has seen many changes during her time at Ballymena Festival. She switched to using an electric piano in 1979, appreciating the lighter touch needed and avoiding the hard work of trying to coax music out of some of the 'old relics' that some festivals offered. She has noted the difference in dancing styles, 'There have been big changes in the dancing styles. Now, even the Under Seven classes are sophisticated. The children seem to progress much quicker and the steps seem much more complicated and difficult. This means I now have to play the music slower so that they can fit in all the extra steps.'

Most of the music played by Rose and her fellow musicians have been well-known for years and she still enjoys some tunes that are 200–300 years old. She has enjoyed her time with Ballymena Festival, even though it is very demanding. 'I enjoy playing for the dancers, although it is very hard, constant work, involving an average of 12 or 13 hours a day.' It is Rose's intention to continue for as long as she is able.

From left, Denis Sweeney, Gerry Kealey and Rose Murray make music together

'I have many happy memories of Ballymena Festival, I've made many friends, and I'm so proud to still be part of it in their Centenary year.'

# Section 3

## 'In their own words'

Any history of Ballymena Festival would be incomplete without hearing from those who have been involved with the Festival over the years. In this section, singers, adjudicators, musicians, teachers and parents, give their impressions of the Festival and of the influence it has had on them.

*Ballymena Festival*

# Elizabeth Bicker
## Adjudicator and Accompanist

My mother, Margaret Bailie, was born in 1916 and in her teens she competed in piano classes in Ballymena. Even in those early years of the Festival, competitors appeared from far and wide. My mother travelled from Dunmurry in those days, and I have three medals which she proudly kept all her life! She often told the story of an unforgettable occasion when, on her way to the platform to play a piano duet with her friend, Eileen, she realised that the elastic of her bloomers had failed. She held grimly on with one hand until they got seated, whereupon both girls had a fit of the giggles at her predicament. They laughed their way through their piece, whereupon the adjudicator, in blissful ignorance of what had happened, commended the girls on showing such evident enjoyment of the music!

I was employed firstly as Official Accompanist in Ballymena and travelled for over twenty years to play in the Town Hall every spring. Life was not easy in the 1970s and 80s but the Festival volunteers worked tirelessly to look after the competitors, supporters and professionals who were involved. There was always a first class piano in the Town Hall and the pride of Ballymena Council and citizens was obvious. My first attempt at adjudication took place at Ballymena Festival and I was invited back to adjudicate several times. The most memorable was in the year of the Festival's return to the Town Hall after its refurbishment, and with typical attention to detail, the Festival Committee managed to purchase a new grand piano.

I am proud to say that former pupils of mine are now involved with Ballymena Festival as teachers of competitors and, in one case, as Official Accompanist.

This continuation of public service is crucial if a Festival is to maintain its standards, and the membership of the Festival Committee is an outstanding example. I have worked in Ballymena with men and women who were full-time teachers, school inspectors, businessmen and women, council officials, civil servants, medical personnel, all of whom have devoted their valuable time and energy to the planning and implementation of this annual event.

With their standards of presentation, care for the competitors, adjudicators and accompanists through difficult times, along with never-failing courtesy and kindness, Ballymena Festival volunteers have set a shining example to the country.

# The McCann family

From an early age, Peggy Neeson had a love for both literature and poetry, and when she married Jack McCann in 1952, their partnership led to many happy years in amateur dramatics producing, directing and performing. Peggy also involved her young family in the arts and for many years, her children attended Mae McCartney's School of Speech and Drama. Like their mother, the McCann children had a flair for performing and for many years they were regular participants at the Festival in Ballymena.

Following Mae McCartney's retirement, Peggy began to tutor her own children along with the children of friends and neighbours. They remained faithful to Ballymena Festival and it became part of McCann family life each February and March. It was a great source of pleasure to Peggy to see her children and her students performing on stage and she embodied the ethos of the Festival as she encouraged everyone to take part, regardless of their success.

Her commitment and dedication to Ballymena Festival continued when she joined the committee. Planning and organising an event as large and as popular as Ballymena Festival requires months of preparation and planning but Peggy was able to accommodate this with ease and aplomb. She developed friendships through her participation on the committee and she continued to support it long after her children had grown up and moved on with their lives.

However, in 1999, Peggy's grandchildren began to perform at the festival, and on many occasions she was on duty at 'the desk' taking their tickets as they nervously waited to say their poem. What a treat for them to have their beloved grandmother announce their names to the adjudicator and audience gathered in the hall!

Happily, the McCanns are continuing with the tradition of verse speaking as two of Peggy's grandsons continue to participate in the Festival each year.

Peggy McCann with grandsons
Joseph and Richard

# The Richards family

Stephen and Mairead Richards with (from left) Eva, Caroline,
Lydia and Athena

The involvement of the four Richards girls in Ballymena Festival kicked off in 1998 with six-year-old Lydia's rendition in the Speech and Drama section of 'Under my bed' by Barbara Ireson. She wasn't placed. But for the next sixteen years, the girls were regularly involved over the different sections and increasingly in the Instrumental section. February was the mad month! As any parent will know, you don't send a child off to prepare themselves and turn up with the finished piece on stage. We listened to hundreds of poems, tunes, duets, quartets on many instruments at all levels from beginner recorder and violin to diploma cello, and to speech performances from 'My Rabbit' (but the pronunciation remained 'My Wabbit'!) to the Programme Class on Elizabeth Jennings.

By 2005, there was a strong string contingent from Broughshane Primary School, enabling the girls to form duets, trios and quartets with school friends for the Festival. As they moved on to Ballymena Academy they formed chamber music groups and helped the Academy to gain considerable success.

Not every performance was a good one. There were the misunderstood poems, the dancing that wasn't 'on the toes' enough and the sisterly 'Train Blues' piano duet that went spectacularly off the rails.

What impact has the annual festival had on the sisters? It has given children with some innate ability the chance to develop into aspiring musicians, with two of them looking to music for a career. But what they all have is a love for music, an understanding of music performance, keenness to make music with others (including a family string quartet) and the confidence to stand on a platform and communicate, whether in words or music. It has given three of them an opportunity to travel to the United States over the last four summers, Caroline to study in Hungary, and all of them to make money from time to time at functions.

Music has become a life choice for Caroline and Eva. Caroline is completing a B Mus Ed degree in Trinity College, Dublin, looking towards a teaching career, while Eva is about the start the second year of a Music Performance Degree in Manchester. Lydia and Athena would not consider music as a career, but Athena spent three weeks in San Diego last summer playing with the Youth Orchestra there.

# The O'Donnell family
## (Shalini, Roshan, Ganesha and Anna-Maria)

Having lived in other countries, we have been amazed at the provision of a world class musical festival on our doorstep. Since our first child took part in 1996, it has become a must to send our children to as many classes as possible.

They have competed in all musical genres (classical, traditional, jazz,) and instruments (piano, recorder, viola, cello, harp, fiddle, saxophone, trumpet and chanter). They have competed in solo classes as well as in duets, trios, choirs and orchestras and have won many prizes, most notably the Claire Hudson trophy, the Alyson Reid trophy and the Durston-Olphert trophy.

Although venues have changed through the years, there was never any loss of quality. The strict, consistent protocol gave discipline and was comforting to the children who eventually learned that a performance was required. They had to leave their shy selves behind and recognise that all the competitors were going through similar experiences. Winning a prize boosted their confidence, most especially if they won a 'Most promising' accolade, because that spurred them on to come back year after year.

Anna Maria and Ganesha O'Donnell

As parents, the festival gave us much entertainment. It has boosted our children's self-esteem and given them the ability to stand up in public. Feedback from the adjudicators has helped them refine and progress with their grade examinations, which has in turn enabled them to enter major orchestras.

We are most grateful to the many great teachers who have taught them over the years, and special thanks go to the late Robert Farren and Denis Sweeney.

Finally, an abiding memory is of seeing our son, Roshan, singing 'O Holy Night' at a Christmas carol service in school. This was done at short notice, never having had a singing lesson, but he excelled entirely because of the skills he had learned at Ballymena Festival.

Eva Richards, currently studying cello performance in Manchester

# Eva Richards

The number one fear in the UK or USA is public speaking. I don't think that is the case for people who have participated in Ballymena Festival! My first performance at the Festival was when I was 5, reciting a poem whose title is now lost to history. As the third of four children, this was potentially the first time that I'd ever been the centre of attention, and I liked it! I wasn't placed, but I continued to enter the Festival for another 13 years, playing the piano, violin, recorder, and ultimately the cello, which became my instrument of choice. Notable memories include a performance of the piano duet 'Train Blues' with my sister Caroline, when I was 7, in which the train completely derailed and came to an embarrassing halt.

The highlight of my Festival career was winning the annual Beggs and Partners Young Instrumentalist of the Year in 2013. This was also the year in which I became Northern Ireland Young Musician of the Year and gained a place in the National Youth Orchestra of Great Britain. After 12 years of looking at this as a goal, I realised that while winning the prize was nice, the exhilaration of performance itself was almost as good a feeling.

For each of the past three summers, I have been given opportunities to travel to the United States. I went first to Minnesota to participate in 'Cello: An American Experience' then to the Apple Hill Center for Chamber Music in New Hampshire for which I was awarded a 'Playing for Peace' scholarship.

I am currently studying Cello Performance at the Royal Northern College of Music - a path I would never have taken if Ballymena Festival had not given me a taste of the exhilaration and emotional involvement that the performance of music enables me to experience. Ballymena Festival, while it does foster and hone competitive instincts, ultimately provides each and every participant with an opportunity to face their fears and to experience the thrill of being onstage.

Johnny Murphy pictured in his shop in Ballymena

# Johnny Murphy
## Fiddle player, teacher and fiddle maker

My life in fiddle competitions started on the stage in Ballymena Town Hall back in 1995, when I was 12 years old. Back then, I was new to everything to do with Traditional music and I remember very well being guided by my uncle, Jim McNeill, over to the adjudicator's table. Sitting at that table was one of the great pillars of the music Festival, Billy McKee, waiting eagerly to hear the new blood. Little did I know that I was in the presence of a respected fiddle player, and someone who would become a lifelong friend.

As time went on, I began to realise how significant the people were who came to that room. There were players like Dennis Sweeney, Dominic McNabb, John Kennedy and many more who became mentors to me and to so many others as we developed our playing.

A very fond memory is of winning the Senior Fiddle Cup for the first time, still in the same room where I started, and with almost all of those present who had witnessed my musical development. When I looked at the names on the cup, names like Kathleen Smyth, Seamus Richmond, Deirdre Shannon, Jim McKillop, Niall Mulligan and other top players,

I was in a state of disbelief. On that day, I realised how important the Traditional section in Ballymena Festival was in the development of the young musicians in the area. Not only has it been a great place for the young to build confidence in performing, but also somewhere for them to make lifelong friends and meet County Antrim's finest.

For me, this Festival has been a fountain of knowledge from the people I have met and the things I have learned. I am proud to say that my own pupils now compete in Ballymena just as I did and they and I look forward to it every year.

Long may the fountain of knowledge flow!

# Maeve Flanagan
## A teacher in St Brigid's Primary School

My first experience of Ballymena Festival began more than 20 years ago when I was 6 years old. I was singing a solo and was so excited that I couldn't sleep the night before my performance. I can remember patiently waiting for my name to be called and the long climb up the stairs to the stage in the large hall - I thought I would never get there! Those familiar feelings of excitement mixed with nerves and butterflies stayed with me throughout my years performing in the Festival.

I looked forward to February every year when I would participate in instrumental, vocal and speech and drama classes. With three sisters also participating in numerous events throughout the week, my Mum would joke about setting up camp in the Town Hall. She did, in fact, have to draw up a timetable for the week and quite literally run up and down the stairs to catch our performances.

The Festival was a very sociable experience. I would go to the Town Hall with my family and friends and meet the same faces year after year. New friendships were formed with other competitors and often we would go for an ice-cream or pick'n'mix at Woolworths with our new friends. As I grew older, each performance brought more nerves, yet the whole experience was extremely enjoyable, and I feel I can attribute many of the valuable life-skills I have acquired to the years standing on the stage at the Town Hall.

My most recent experiences of the Festival have been from a completely different perspective - that of the teacher - a position I have found to be the most anxious of all. I want every child to enjoy the experience and perform to the best of their ability, whether it is remembering words, having the confidence to sing in front of others or winning a prize. Fortunately, the adjudicators and Festival Committee members are always on hand to do whatever they can to help every child succeed. Through the years, I have had the pleasure of watching children grow in confidence and self-esteem, making all the nerves and months of hard work worthwhile. I would like to take this opportunity to thank the Festival Committee for all of their hard work and support throughout the years.

# Phoebe McDonald
## School teacher at St Colmcille's Primary School

My association with Ballymena Festival started back in 1975. As a pupil of the late Mrs Mary Barr, the festival was the highlight of the year for me, not least because having been entered in so many classes, it meant almost a whole week off school.

My family's association with the Festival, however, goes back much further. My late mother, Eileen Robinson, (nee McCrystal) had also been a pupil of Mrs Barr and had competed very successfully throughout the 40s and 50s.

However, I did not experience the same success in my years of competing in solo classes. I was one of those people who, wracked with nerves, was rarely able to perform to the standard required to win a prize. I distinctly recall, one year, being so nervous that I was unable to get off the chair, let alone make it onto the stage! I always admired my sister, Dawn, who could breeze onto the platform year after year, frequently being awarded 100% for her solo sight-singing endeavours.

I competed in the vocal and instrumental sections from age 7-17 but what I loved most was our choir performances. Choral music still

Mrs Barr's Albert choristers seen with their trophies in 1978

remains my passion. I say with great pride that I was a member of the Albert Chorus, so named because we rehearsed in Albert Place in the town. I recall so many of us in Mrs Barr's loft above her garage, preparing for Festival week, that it could only have been a miracle that we didn't fall into the garage below. Unlike now, Health and Safety and Child Protection weren't top of the agenda in those days! Then, in the week before the Festival, we were all marched to St Patrick's Hall, Castle Street, to practise walking on and off stage.

In 1985, I took part in my last competition as a pupil and began entering my own pupils, proudly supported by both my parents. This began with our Parish Folk Group of All Saints, who competed successfully for almost 20 years. When I began teaching in St Louis' Primary, I almost felt as if I had taken over from Mrs Barr, who by this stage had retired. This continued with the opening of St Colmcille's Primary, where I still teach.

My own children have experienced the Festival since shortly after they were born. Michael, now 17, was only 6 weeks old when he first lay silently in my arms, for hours at a time, while my own pupils took part. He was never interested in performing on stage. He preferred the job of helping Mrs Collie collect the competitors' tickets or helping Ian (Craig) to man the door. The promise of a sausage supper at lunch was enough to hold his attention for hours. He looked forward to getting his good shirt and tie on for Gala night although he would have preferred it if I'd let him wear a suit and dickey-bow as he wanted to look like one of the Committee! Rebecca, now 14, was different. At the age of 3, she sang in the under 12 Folk Song Class (should I mention that she sang the same verse of 'I'll tell me ma' 3 times?). She has taken part in Vocal, Instrumental and Speech and Drama sections of the Festival and loves any chance to perform. Her favourite part of the Gala night each year was to award marks to the female competitors for their dress and hairstyle. Singing wasn't at all important!

Further family involvement in the Festival comes with my eldest sister, Mary, who has been heavily involved in the Dance section as a teacher of the Seven Towers School of Dancing.

From 2005-2010, I had the privilege of being a member of the Festival Committee. This time was an eye-opener to me as I witnessed the dedication of people who gave so freely of their time and energy to give our children a chance to showcase their talent. So much of their work goes unnoticed. Apart from what we see taking place at the Festival, months of voluntary work goes on behind the scenes, planning and organising, in order to keep the Festival, now one of the biggest in Europe, running smoothly. As I write this, I think fondly of those members no longer with us.

So, what are some of the things that stand out most to me about the Festival? Firstly, the warm welcome received year after year; the friendly faces of Philip, Frances, Marjorie and the team who made endless tea and coffee in the old Town Hall tuck shop; the lifelong friendships I have made through the Festival; the standard of performances which gets better every year; the focus on taking part, not the winning, the pride felt by the children (and the parents) when they have been able to overcome nerves and apprehension and step on stage to do their bit; the look of relief on faces when the performance is finished; the tears, thankfully not often, when a performance hasn't gone so well; the look of surprise on faces who weren't expecting to win; the 'special' performances that took place beside the adjudicator's table when a child was too nervous to get onto the platform; performances of a standard that made the hairs on the back of my neck stand on end... the list goes on and on. But out of my forty years' involvement in the Festival as competitor, teacher and parent, what are the memories that stand out the most to me?

One such memory is Mrs Dorothy Collie, down on one knee on the stage, beside a small child with learning difficulties, as he tried to remember the words of his song. Another, much more recent, is one of my own pupils with learning difficulties, who was unable to read any of the words on the page, but had managed to learn six songs off by heart. He not only competed as part of our school choir, but to my absolute delight, also took part in the vocal solo class.

Finally, a performance given by a local special school, not the most tuneful I'd ever heard, but that didn't matter. It was a performance that resulted in not a dry eye in the house, and for which the choir won the Don Robinson Cup, presented to the Festival in memory of my father. For me, that's what the Festival is all about and that's what a performer strives for - to stir the emotions of the listener and create a memory that lasts.

As the Ballymena Festival celebrates its 100th anniversary, I would like to offer my congratulations and best wishes for its future success. But I also offer my thanks to all the people over the years who have helped to make it what it is today and for the huge part it has played in my life over the past 40 years. I would also like to encourage our local children, schools and teachers to continue to participate with enthusiasm each year, and to remember, with genuine sincerity, it's not the winning but the taking part that counts.

Wishing God's blessing to you all.

Stephen Rankin prepares for
another performance

# Stephen Rankin

I am Stephen Rankin from Ballymena, currently studying music at the
Royal Conservatoire in Glasgow.

When I was 11 years old, my flute tutor, Mr Glen Houston, encouraged
me to enter Ballymena Festival. I entered the 'Flute solo class, 12 years
and under' category and I gained first place. This was such a thrill as it
was one of my first public performances at such a young age.

I realised I had the potential to succeed and quickly discovered that
I loved performing in front of an audience. I continued to work hard,
and with much practice and guidance from my flute tutor, I progressed
through graded exams, gaining my Associate, Licentiate and Fellowship
performance Diplomas.

I have absolutely no doubt that performing on the stage at Ballymena
Festival has been a valuable experience in a number of ways; firstly, by
gaining invaluable confidence and experience performing in front of an
audience, as well as benefitting greatly from the comments and advice
given by the various adjudicators. Moreover, the committee members
and volunteers of the Festival have always been most welcoming and

encouraging. Not only this, the festival has given me the opportunity to compete against a great many very talented musicians, many of whom have become great friends with whom I still keep in contact.

The highlight of my career at the Festival came in 2011, when I won the Beggs and Partners 'Young Instrumentalist of the year' award. As a resident of Ballymena, performing at the Festival has always been special and I consider it an honour to compete and showcase my abilities in my local area.

Ballymena Festival of Music, Speech and Dance is a great opportunity to encourage young people to develop their talents, to continue to practise, to make progress in their specialism and to increase their confidence. I have very fond memories of my performances in the music classes at the Festival and am very grateful for all the support and encouragement given to me.

# Rachel Thompson

My name is Rachel Thompson (née Mol) and I am a professional soprano based in the Netherlands. I have toured all over the world with Irish and Dutch choirs in addition to working with NI Opera and my busy solo schedule.

My association with Ballymena Festival began when I was just five, with my first climb up what seemed like enormous steps to the platform to sing a song about a Friendly Cow!

I competed each year until I left university - and the friendships I made, the advice I received and the performing experience I gained at the Festival still influence my professional life today.

The Festival provides a wonderful opportunity for young people to hone their skills in a supportive environment - an opportunity for which I am most grateful.

*The following is an extract from a report written in 1966 by a 10 year-old pupil from Lisnamurrican Primary School. It appeared in a little typewritten school magazine and it tells the story from a child's perspective*

# Ballymena Musical Festival

'On Thursday the 17th of February we went into the Ballymena Musical Festival to play our recorders. Mr Nesbitt took his car, Mrs Simpson took hers, and Mummy took ours. All the boys went in Mrs Simpson's car except Trevor Turtle who went in our car with Margaret Nesbitt, Cherith Simpson and me. Mr Nesbitt took Margaret Martin, Billy Connor, Mrs McNabney and Lorna McGregor.

We were in the Town Hall first and about ten minutes later the rest of them came.

Before the Festival we did a lot of rehearsing and hoped we would do well, but we knew we were against a lot of other schools. There were thirty eight entered for the Solos. There were quite a lot of girls from Ballymena County Primary and one boy from Larne and about sixteen or seventeen from our school.

We all sat up towards the front of the hall, and Mr Nesbitt took copies of our music and gave them to the Adjudicator. When it was time to start the Adjudicator said, ''Now we will start.'' Then we each went up in turn and played our pieces and Mrs Simpson accompanied us on the piano. While we were playing, the Adjudicator was writing down our remarks. When everyone had finished playing, the Adjudicator went up to the platform and said what a great performance we had given. He started to give out the marks. As he was reading them out, he left some out. These were the first, second and third. David Thompson of Larne got first and the Adjudicator said that this showed what could be done with a recorder. He got 90%. Emily Connor of our school got second with 88%. A girl from County Primary, Dermott Simpson and I got third with 85 marks. We each got badges and were very pleased. After this, Mr Nesbitt took us all to the Lido to have lunch.

At two o'clock, we were to play again. In this class the County Primary, a Larne group, one from Antrim and Lisnamurrican were entered. The

Antrim group didn't turn up. We played first, the County Primary next and the Larne Group of four boys last. The boys from Larne got first with 90 marks. We got second with 85 marks. Everybody was overjoyed because we all got badges.

Then we all came back to school, and Mr Nesbitt gave us our papers and he was very pleased with us for our first performance.'

# The McCloskey family

For many years I have sat at Ballymena Festival Traditional music days, firstly as a participant, then as a teacher and finally as a parent. People would often comment, "Gosh, that was a long, tiring day for you.", but actually it never really felt either long or tiring, probably because I was enjoying the great music and was full of admiration for the many young people, including our own children, who were taking part.

My father, Jimmy Logan, was a Ballymena man and it was he who first brought me to the Town Hall on Traditional day. I remember getting up onto a huge stage and looking up at the amazing ceiling of the main hall - sure it might as well have been Carnegie Hall! Before long I was bringing my little sister, Aileen Logan, to the festival. By this time the Traditional day had moved to the Civic Chamber. I was an accordion player, so I generally had only one competition, but my sister was a fiddle player and, well, the sky was the limit because she entered and usually won many competitions. One of the big fiddle competitions was, of course, The Michael McIlhatton trophy. Aileen won this no fewer than four times and then went on to watch her pupils, Michael Og and Roisin win it too. Aileen won all the major fiddle competitions at BMF from 1997-2004, a remarkable achievement. She is and continues to be a stalwart of traditional music.

By the time Aileen was retiring from the competitions, she was coming along to support our family, The McCloskeys. We have taken part in many sections of the festival but we are usually associated with Traditional Music. There is Michael Og, Roisin, Owen Colleen, Katie-Anne and the "littlest", Erin (6) who hopes to take part this year for the first time. In different combinations, they play bodhran, fiddle, harp, flute and saxophone, and not forgetting tin whistle.

All the family have had great success over the years but I suppose it was Roisin's big win of 'The Sandy Spence Shield for the Most Promising Tin whistle Player' back in 2002 that got us really hooked. Yes! That was well spotted by the adjudicator that day, as Roisin has gone on to win several All-Ireland Tin whistle titles and has earned initials of DipLCM, ALCM and TTCT, all on the Tin Whistle.

The McCloskey Family with some of their
many trophies

Traditional day at Ballymena festival started off as a fun day in February, when you would go play a tune, then go shopping but as the number of instruments, competitions and children grew, the shopping day had to be put off to a full day of its own. However that didn't dampen spirits and every year, everyone would look forward to the next festival. While not all the family compete any more, the competitions hold a great place in everyone's heart. It has not only taught the children a great discipline but has developed respect and courtesy, and a sense of achievement that will remain with them for the rest of their lives.

I'm sure the original committee never imagined that they would have such far reaching influence on the young people of the 21st century.

# Lucy Spong (née Close)
## 'Toffee's chewy, treacle's gooey, ice-cream's licky, honey's sticky. . .'

No, not Shakespeare or Heaney, but the opening lines of my first poem at Ballymena Festival. I was aged four, and my tiny heart was pounding. Mrs Kathleen Regan, our neighbour and a Festival committee member, had persuaded Mum that I should take part. Those lines have been repeated often in the Close household ever since, usually with the intention of embarrassing me!

In the ten years that I took part in the Festival, I learned so much; the poems, drama pieces, readings, quick studies and songs. Every year before competitions I would trot up to the Regans to say my piece and wait for advice or approval. I met, and was helped by, many wonderful people along the way. I owe a great debt of gratitude to people like Kathleen Regan, Mary Kearney who prepared me for Speech and Drama, and Noreen Law who coached me for singing competitions. I suppose I was stage-struck from the very beginning, and the experience not only gave me a love of the arts but also shaped my career in the theatre.

Lucy Close with Speech and
Drama cups

And the memories… I will never forget the first Monday mornings of the Festival. There was always a brand new programme, hot off the press. I recall the excitement of highlighting my name and my friends' names in the various competitions. The nerves jangling, the smell of polish in the Town Hall, the clinking of tea cups … and then the hush as Mrs May Matthews announced the first competition – and we were off! Getting out of school and a week of doing things I loved every day, whether performing or just watching others. The nail-biting as the results were announced – and that was just the mums!

In the drama competitions I was able to dress up as characters as various as Verucca Salt, Lady Jane Grey and Anne Frank. My recollection of the latter enabled me to sound knowledgeable about Nazi crimes in Amsterdam and occupied Europe in 1944, in a GCSE history exam.

It was in Ballymena Festival events that I encountered some great writing, whether it was Yeats' love poems, the humour in T S Eliot's 'Macavity' or the beauty and pathos of John Hewitt's 'Cushkib Fair'. The confidence I gained in the Festival enabled me to go to the 75th anniversary celebration of the British and International Federation of Festivals of Music, Dance and Speech in Warwick as the youngest competitor from Northern Ireland. I was thirteen, and proud to come back with a gold medal for my presentation of poems by Seamus Heaney, a memory I shall always treasure.

Lucy was the youngest solo performer to win
a gold medal at the Festival of Festivals in Warwick

Some competitions went well, some not so well. There was the time I started my song with the third verse. 'Oops,' quoth I, and asked the accompanist to start again. I had to settle for a bronze that time. Or when I forgot my lines in a drama piece and had to improvise. Ad-libbing was a skill we had to practise later at drama school. The Festival experience served me then and throughout my career in acting. Whether to win or to lose, but to do so with grace, was one of the most important lessons learnt.

That, and self-confidence. Standing up on a stage before an audience from an early age and delivering a poem, a piece of drama, or belting out a song – that was a priceless experience. Not only do you learn to conquer your nerves, but what could be an ordeal becomes a challenge and ultimately a pleasure.

Another vital skill was developed in the quick study competitions. Reading something quickly and under pressure was an invaluable lesson which stood me in good stead when it came to auditions. You could look at the script, but you also had to make eye-contact with your audience. This is a transferable skill which has proved useful in my career in theatre management, recently at the Theatre Royal Drury Lane, and now at the South Bank Complex.

I live in London now but still love to hear how everything is going at Ballymena Festival. I hope that it continues for many years to give every child the opportunity to experience, learn and enjoy as much as I did.

Is there another little four year-old out there learning the words of 'Toffee's chewy...'?

I hope so.

Marilynne Davies has visited Ballymena
regularly as vocal and instrumental adjudicator

# Marilynne Davies
## Adjudicator

'The thing about performance is that is a CELEBRATION of the fact that we DO contain within ourselves infinite possibilities'

For the past 100 years Ballymena Festival has provided a platform for performers to realise these 'infinite possibilities'

The Music section of the Festival has always provided a wide range of classes across the age range so that individuals, or small and large groups of performers can participate whether as soloists, a member of an African drumming group, or a choir or orchestra.

In my experience, performances in the Music section of Ballymena Festival have always reached a high standard and that reputation has encouraged performers to come from a wide geographical area to participate.

On my first visit to Ballymena, it was clear that those involved were proud of this reputation and were anxious to protect and develop it further. Valuable links were developed with the various Schools of Music, universities and Conservatoires across Ireland and these proved to be very fruitful. However, with such high expectations of performers comes equally high expectations of Adjudicators – always an unnerving and daunting prospect!

The challenge to any Festival is to balance the encouragement of high standards of performance with the provision of a supportive and non-threatening atmosphere so that everyone, regardless of the stage of musical development, can feel valued and appreciated. In such an atmosphere, everyone will give of their best, and the occasion will be enjoyed by both performer, audience and adjudicator. Ballymena Festival skilfully aims to combine a warm, caring and welcoming atmosphere with high expectations, and they succeed.

From each visit to Ballymena Festival, I have taken away memories of many memorable performances and it has been a joy to follow some of these performers as they move forward in their careers to become successful professional musicians. I recall hearing one of the pianists from Ballymena Festival in the BBC Young Musician of the Year Keyboard Final, and only recently it was a delight to welcome as a soloist one of the singers I had heard in Ballymena. Such is the platform and the opportunity that the Festival provides.

As Ballymena Festival moves forward into the next 100 years, there will be many and varied challenges which reflect the changes in society and in expectations. However, I am sure that the Festival is strong and capable enough to accept such challenges and grow and develop in its response.

Many congratulations on the first 100 years and every good wish for the next 100!

# Anne McCambridge

I was just six years old when I first left my seat in Ballymena Town Hall, walked up the creaky steps, holding on to the handrail, over to an ever-smiling Elizabeth Bicker, the accompanist. There I stood in my favourite dress, knees trembling and butterflies in my tummy. I looked out into the audience at the adjudicator, and the music started.

Anne McCambridge, music educator, director and performer

> *'Oh the Hawthorne tree is a fairy tree, and an evergreen is the Yew,*
> *But I wouldn't cut down the twisted thorns in the mountainy field, would you?'*

It is more than thirty years ago now, and the little song was over almost before I knew it, but it is burned into my memory forever, because I had just survived my first proper performance! I didn't know it then, but this was to be my first step into a musical life, my first medal (third place!) and the first of many platforms, but as a child, Ballymena was always my favourite, my musical home.

I remember Mrs and Mrs Collie, Mrs Regan, Sam Hughes and a whole army of smiling volunteers who were endlessly encouraging and supportive of everyone during times of musical triumph and disaster. Our accompanists, Elizabeth Bicker and Audrey Gillian were with us every step, covering every stumble. Of course, looking back, this would have been in the 1980s at the heart of the Troubles, a difficult time. The Festival was a haven from that, religion and politics had no place within those walls. It did not matter that my school uniform was a different colour, in fact, I felt special there, not different.

I was fortunate to be taught by the indomitable Mrs Mary Barr, a force of nature and a terror if she didn't think that you were doing your very best. Her standards were high, uncompromising and inspirational. I still quote her sometimes with my own students, when she used to stamp her foot and say in exasperation, 'Would you ever go home tonight and pray to God to give you imagination?!' I tend to leave out the foot stamping, but she was absolutely right. Any performance, no matter how beautifully delivered, just doesn't work without it. Mrs Barr crammed so many children into her tiny music room above the garage at Albert Place that it seemed like some kind of musical Tardis. I can't imagine that Health and Safety legislation would allow it these days, but we survived and thrived.

These days I feel blessed to have encountered such welcoming, special and encouraging people so early in my musical life. Ballymena Festival was formative to me as a performer, educator and musical director. Without the experiences I had there, I don't think that I would have had the confidence to step out into the musical world and make my life there. For this I will be forever grateful.

# Alyson Reid
## Music teacher and accompanist

Ballymena Festival holds very special and fond memories for me. My first affiliation was as a young, local piano teacher, eager to learn her craft from professional adjudicators, and the irreplaceable lessons of practical experience. As every child steps onto the platform of this festival, they grow in maturity and competence (and so do the teachers and parents). Nothing is wasted – even the mistakes are a positive learning experience.

Ballymena Festival was always friendly, encouraging and welcoming. As I grew into the role of festival accompanist, I have such great memories of performances partnering the very young and those more seasoned in their craft. I well remember playing for huge classes of 50 young voices, all singing songs like 'The bright umbrella', while Dorothy Collie and I gleefully assembled a colourful umbrella beside the piano for fun. There were many other props, ranging from cuddly toys to a home-made scarecrow! We always tried to make the young ones smile and relax so they could engage and give of their best.

There were, of course, many good-hearted laughs behind the scenes too, such as the reply from one young lady when asked what tempo she preferred for her song. The reply came in a thick Ulster dialect, 'Nae tae fast and nae tae slow!'

My most favourite accompaniment moment, I think, was partnering Carolyn Dobbin as she silenced the audience in awe as she sang Schubert's 'Du bist die Ruh'. It was simply sublime and an honour to be a part of such beauty in music.

I will be forever grateful to have been mentored by Elizabeth Bicker as she was so encouraging and generous in sharing her talent. I will always be thankful to Audrey Gillian who kept me sane when difficult music arrived to the platform tattered, torn and maybe not having the correct numbers of pages!

These days my role has changed to supporting as a mum, and watching the legacy unfold for the next generation. I salute all who have faithfully served Ballymena Festival over the years, and celebrate, with you, its continued success.

# APPENDICES

Appendix A
> A list of Office-bearers 2016 together with a description of
> their duties

Appendix B
> An overview of each Festival section
> Instrumental music
> Vocal music
> Speech and Drama
> Traditional Dance
> Traditional Music
> Modern Dance

Appendix C
> Trophies at Ballymena Festival

Appendix D
> Ballymena Festival and the World Wide Web

Appendix E
> Adjudicators at Ballymena Festival 1916-2016
> Sir Hugh Roberton, Tyrone Guthrie, Laurence Binyon,
> Dr Havelock Nelson
>
> Instrumental music
> Vocal music
> Speech and Drama
> Traditional music
> Ballet
> Modern Dance
> Traditional Dance

# APPENDIX A
## Ballymena Festival of Music, Speech and Dance Office Bearers 2016

President: Mrs Irene Cumming
Chairman: Mr Stanley Hughes
Vice-Chairmen: Miss Joyce Coulter and Dr Andrew Hudson
General Secretary: Miss Joyce Coulter
Assistant Secretary: Mr David Loughridge
Membership Secretary: Mrs Mary Campbell
Treasurer: Mrs Mandy Boyd
Catering Secretary: Miss Isobel Halliday
Cups and Trophies Secretary: Mrs Isobel Petticrew
Safeguarding Officer: Mrs Ruth Orr
Chief Steward and Health and Safety Officer: Mr Geoff Orr
Publicity Secretary: Mrs Delia Close

SECTION SECRETARIES
Vocal music Secretary: Mrs Dorothy Collie
Assistant vocal music Secretary: Mr Alan Forster
Instrumental music Secretary: Mrs Mairead Richards
Accompanist Secretary: Mrs Rae Shiels
Traditional music Secretary: Mrs Anne-Marie McCloskey
Irish dance Secretary: Mrs Regina McNeill
Modern dance Secretary: Mrs Angela Morrow
Speech and drama Secretary: Mrs Hazel Bonar

A list of names and titles gives only the bare minimum of information; it does not tell what any of the office bearers actually does before, during and after each festival. Those who attend the festival as audience members may have no idea that some of the posts exist and they will definitely not know what some of the posts entail. Without going into laborious detail, the following summarises what each role contributes to the smooth running of the festival every year.

The PRESIDENT acts as a figurehead for the whole organisation. The President will attend committee meetings, will attend as many festival sessions as possible, and will be on hand on Gala evenings to greet special guests and sponsors. The President will also represent the festival at other functions.

The CHAIRMAN takes charge of committee meetings, ensuring they are conducted properly and efficiently. The Chairman is responsible for liaising with external bodies, including the council and various sponsors. The Chairman normally acts as compere on Gala evenings and will also be present to open and close the various sections.

VICE-CHAIRMEN assist the Chairman in the various roles, chairing meetings if the Chairman is unavailable and accompanying the Chairman to external meetings.

The GENERAL SECRETARY works closely with the Chairman in drawing up agendas for meetings and is responsible for making sure that minutes are taken. The General Secretary deals with correspondence and is in contact with Federation Headquarters to ensure that Ballymena conforms to the necessary regulations. The General Secretary is also responsible for drawing up rotas to cover platform and adjudicator stewarding duties during the festival.
If the General Secretary is unable to attend any Committee Meetings, the ASSISTANT GENERAL SECRETARY will take minutes and deal with correspondence.

The MEMBERSHIP SECRETARY issues annual membership letters and keeps control of season tickets. The Membership secretary ensures that members are notified of upcoming meetings and assists in organising where the meetings are to be held.

The TREASURER ensures that accurate accounts are kept of money received and money paid out. The Treasurer is responsible for the system of gathering and banking cash received during the festival. The Treasurer has the responsibility of paying bills for expenses incurred in the running of the festival.

During the Festival the CATERING SECRETARY recruits and organises a number of volunteers to provide and serve food at break times to adjudicators, stewards and officers. It is impossible to overstate how important this is for all those who benefit from the tea-breaks in the morning, afternoon and evening schedules. Apart from the bonus of the food and drink, the opportunity to chat and relax for a short time is very welcome and much appreciated by all.

The CUPS AND TROPHIES SECRETARY is responsible for the safe-keeping of the many cups and trophies that have been presented to Ballymena Festival over the years. The cups must be accurately catalogued and those which are not being presented are stored securely. Each year, the Cups Secretary has to request the return of trophies won the previous year. These must be collected, examined, cleaned and/or repaired if necessary and made ready for being presented again. The Cups Secretary brings the relevant cups to the room where the class is taking place on each day of the Festival. It is a huge task especially since the Festival runs over several weeks.

The SAFEGUARDING OFFICER must ensure that Ballymena Festival keeps abreast of the requirements laid down in legislation regarding the safeguarding of young people and vulnerable adults. The Safeguarding Officer will liaise with bodies such as PSNI and the British Federation of Festivals and will make sure that the policies adopted by the Festival are understood and implemented by all volunteers. The Safeguarding Officer will make sure that a check is kept on the movements of volunteers during the festival and will record any incidents or problems.

The CHIEF STEWARD AND HEALTH AND SAFETY OFFICER organises and trains volunteers to act as stewards during the festival. The stewards are responsible for taking ticket money, directing audience members to the various classes and ensuring that doors are not opened during performances. Any health and safety concerns will be noted by the officer and dealt with as quickly as possible.

The PUBLICITY SECRETARY aims to ensure that as many people as possible know about the Festival, when it is on and what may be seen. The Publicity secretary will liaise with the local papers to enable them to print timely articles. The Publicity secretary will also organise photo calls with photographers from the local papers to cover the launch of the new syllabus as well as recording various prize-winners during the festival.

The SECTION SECRETARIES must make all the necessary arrangements to ensure that the various classes run smoothly. The Secretary will book an appropriate adjudicator and will liaise with the adjudicator to decide what will appear in the syllabus for the new festival. The section secretary will use the festival website to update the syllabus. The secretary will deal with entries coming in either by post or online. When entries are declared closed, the programme for the section must be worked out then entered on the website. The secretary will either e-mail or post call-sheets detailing when and where classes will take place and will deal with phone enquiries about late entries or scheduling problems. Adjudication sheets must be printed for every class. Music secretaries will ensure that the music is available for the adjudicator to follow and that accompanists have the correct music. Secretaries for dance sections will organise musical accompaniment for the dancers. Badges and certificates must be prepared and the secretary must help to organise those who volunteer as platform or adjudicator stewards. The section secretary will collect the adjudicator and ensure they are settled in their hotel and that they are happy with the arrangements. During the festival, the secretaries will be on hand to deal with any queries and will make sure that results are recorded so that they can be entered on the festival website.

These are not paid positions. The only people who receive any remuneration from Ballymena Festival are the adjudicators and accompanists who do such an outstanding job. Everyone else works on a voluntary basis just as they have been doing since 1916 when the Festival began.

# APPENDIX B
## Section overview

When Ballymena Festival started in May 1916, there were only two disciplines. Instrumental music was represented by piano and Vocal Music covered solos, duets and choirs. Over the years, other disciplines have joined and in 2016, the Festival will be made up of six distinct sections, all of which are organised on an individual basis by the relevant section secretary. This is not to say that the sections focus solely on themselves. In fact, there is a great degree of cooperation and camaraderie with everyone helping each other as far as possible. There is certainly no sense of competition between the sections and those organising the Festival are always impressed by the level of skill and talent shown by performers in the different disciplines. Of course, there will be some children who take part in more than one section so the weeks of the Festival are busy for them and their parents. There will be days when Instrumental, Vocal and Speech and Drama classes are all happening at The Braid; this can sometimes cause complications where a child is required in two places at one time, but provided that the section secretary is informed of the problem, provision will always be made for a child to be heard either earlier or later than stated in the programme. This was not always the case because in looking back at old programmes, it is interesting to note the warnings that anyone who was 'late' had to explain themselves to the chairman himself and only <u>he</u> could decide if they would be allowed to perform!

The following is a brief overview of the individual sections.

# Instrumental music

Instrumental music was one of the foundation sections in Ballymena Musical Festival, although for many years, only piano and violin were heard in the competitions. It was not until the 1960s that the section began to expand, first with flutes, then with brass instruments until finally the section now caters for people of all ages playing all kinds of instruments. Indeed, a new class for 'Tuned and Untuned Percussion' was created so that the hand-bell ringers from St Patrick's Church could take part.

The adjudicator for Instrumental music in Ballymena will hear a vast array of performers playing many different instruments with varying degrees of skill. Over the course of the competitions, the child playing a recorder or junior violin ('wee strings' as it is affectionately known in the Festival) will give way to primary and post-primary school orchestras, the children playing piano duets will be succeeded by the brilliance shown by those taking part in the piano concerto competition. Each performer will receive encouragement and constructive criticism so that the performance can continue to improve.

Successive section secretaries in Instrumental music have worked hard to ensure that the section continues to thrive. Thanks to sponsorship, attractive prizes are now offered to the Instrumentalist of the Year, the Junior Instrumentalist of the Year and the Primary Instrumentalist of the Year. The standard of playing improves every year, and the audience who attend the Instrumental Gala at the end of the week's competitions, are treated to breathtaking music, especially notable since all of those taking part are amateurs.

In 2015, there were well over 400 entries in this section, causing some problems in trying to fit all the classes into the time available. There are worse problems to have, of course, and the fact that the programme is so full is testament to the commitment of organisers, music teachers and, of course, the performers themselves.

# Vocal Music

A long with Instrumental classes, Vocal music was one of the founding disciplines in Ballymena Music Festival. The Festival provided a platform for all sorts of voices, ranging from the junior soloists, through the various choirs, taking in the duettists and not forgetting the trained voices, some of whom were destined for a career in music. Today the Festival still caters for those who wish to sing, whether in serious competition or in non-competitive singing, where enjoyment of the camaraderie of singing is the most important thing.

Vocal music was extremely popular through the early years of the Festival, and the choirs of the factories and mills were to the fore in their enthusiasm. Nowadays there are fewer adult choirs, but they do still come to perform. School choirs are very well represented at Ballymena Festival and there are classes for Primary school, post-primary and special schools. The UTV production 'School Choir of the Year' ran from 1996 - 2005 and during its run it inspired and encouraged many school choirs to go the extra mile in ensuring that they delivered the very best performances they could. There are also non-competitive classes, designed to encourage those taking part to simply enjoy making music together.

Vocal music classes for soloists range from classes for children under 5 right through to the prestigious competitions for male and female voice. The competitions for the latter usually feature in the Final Night Gala, when beautiful singing is combined with some glitz and glamour. Even the men dress in their best.

It is amusing to look back at the programmes for the individual competitions in the early years of the Festival. It was normal for the words of all the set songs to be printed in full; the words of 'Jerusalem' by Parry were always printed as well. This was because every session of the Festival ended with a rendition of 'Jerusalem' by the audience. It is also interesting to note that the music for 'Jerusalem' is printed in staff notation and in tonic sol fa. The requirements for some of the early vocal classes assumed that tonic sol fa would be used. However, in 1937, Dr Staton, the vocal adjudicator, objected strongly to the assumption that choirs and vocalists should learn only tonic sol fa and was reported as saying,

> *'No song, except of the cheapest type was ever set to tonic sol-fa. Tonic sol-fa was the most useful thing in the world to start with but it should be applied to staff notation. Nearly all songs were written in staff notation and there were thousands of modern choral works for which there was no tonic sol-fa notation whatever. Start with tonic sol-fa by all means but do not stop there. Go on to staff notation.'*

As with Instrumental music, entry numbers in the 2015 Festival were very healthy, with over 400 entries received. Extra classes had to be slotted into the programme to cope with the demand. Audience numbers are not as good as they once were, although on school choir days, it is sometimes very difficult to accommodate everyone in the auditorium.

It is impossible to imagine Ballymena Festival without singing and the pleasure it brings to the singers and hearers alike.

# Speech and Drama

Speech and Drama began life in Ballymena Festival as 'Elocution', becoming 'Verse-speaking and dramatic interpretation' for a number of years before finally settling with its current title. This section was added to the Festival at the suggestion of a vocal music adjudicator, who felt that it would benefit the singers in pronouncing their words with clarity. From a modest start of 3 classes in 1924, Speech and Drama has expanded until it now lasts 8 days and sometimes 3 sessions per day. In 2015, there were 1042 entries with children as young as 4 taking part and entries from Belfast, Magherafelt and Antrim as well as Ballymena and the local area.

Visiting adjudicators have always emphasised that they do not insist on an artificial way of speaking and they certainly do not demand BBC English. Mrs Hilda Taggart in the 1960s expressed her feelings to Speech and Drama competitors,

> *'Never be ashamed of where you come from. Good speech training will never, never spoil your own intonation. We don't want you all to be patterns of someone else. We want you to speak with individuality, with your own intonation but clearly and distinctly.'*

The majority of present-day performers in Ballymena Festival's Speech and Drama section come from the local schools, with the Primary school classes being especially popular. The children are taught their poem in school by their teacher, with parents and grandparents forming an appreciative and occasionally anxious audience at the Festival. The junior and senior choral speaking classes are always a highlight of the section with the auditorium filled with school groups, eager to show the adjudicator and audience alike the result of many hours of rehearsal. It is always interesting to see how the various groups interpret the same poem in very different ways.

Speech and Drama in Ballymena also offers competitions for privately taught pupils, ranging from verse-speaking to quick study and from prose classes to drama. Many of the performers take part in several classes, so the days of the Festival are busy and demanding for everyone concerned.

Adjudicators are always very complimentary about the high standard of the work that they see and hear. This is testament to the excellent work done by teachers and to the dedication of their pupils.

# Traditional dance

Traditional dance began life in Ballymena Festival as 'Folk-dancing' and it first appeared on the syllabus of the Festival in the late 1920s. At that time and for many years after, folk-dancing encompassed Scottish dancing as well as traditional Irish dancing. Once folk-dancing was introduced to the festival, it quickly became very popular indeed and the numbers involved meant that the section demanded more and more time to allow everyone to participate. It has continued to be the section with the highest number of entries, drawing in dancers who fill the Town Hall with colour and enthusiasm at the very start of the Festival in February.

In Ballymena, a number of dancing schools send their pupils along to compete with each other every year. All will be members of the Festival Dance Teachers Association which grew out of the Nine Glens Association formed in 1971 to champion the style of dancing known

Patricia Mulholland was a noted traditional dance teacher and instrumentalist
*Image from Patricia Mulholland Collection, courtesy of the National Dance Archives of Ireland at the University of Limerick, Glucksman Library*

as Festival rather than Feis dancing. Festival dancing style has been heavily influenced by Patricia Mulholland who was passionate about Irish dancing being made accessible to all sections of the community and who also promoted a more lyrical and expressive type of dancing. Festival dance teachers encourage each dancer to express their unique movement, interpreting the narrative of the music.

In many ways, Festival dancing represents a model of cultural integration with all sections of the community being involved at all levels in the movement.

It is a huge task to cope with the numbers of dancers taking part, with ages ranging from the very young to young adults. In the days before the refurbishment of the Town Hall, dancing took place on the floor of the auditorium, whereas nowadays the platform is used. Music is performed live with traditional musicians working hard to keep up with the flying feet.

There is no sign of the appeal of Festival dancing waning so that Ballymena Festival can continue to play host to enthusiastic and dedicated performers in this exhilarating discipline.

# Traditional music

Traditional music has evolved in Ballymena Festival from being one class tacked onto the instrumental section to being a complete section in its own right. It started life as 'Country fiddling' and for many years it took place on a Friday night, rollicking into the small hours of the Saturday morning. It was always one of the most popular sessions, taking on a very different atmosphere to some of the more staid competitions.

There were problems, though, because the instrumental adjudicator, classically trained and used to certain techniques, often found himself in great difficulties in being able to pronounce on the very different techniques employed by the fiddlers. It may well have been Havelock Nelson who, according to the story told by eyewitnesses, had to be smuggled out by the back door after his adjudication had aroused the fury of the fiddling experts in the audience.

The wise decision was taken to use an expert to adjudicate the country fiddling from then on. It was not until the 1960s that the section expanded to take in other instruments and today, a wide variety of instruments are played during the Saturday devoted to traditional music. It is also notable how many young people are involved, many with amazing levels of expertise despite their youth. Again, the devotion of teachers and the dedication of their pupils is demonstrated very clearly throughout all the classes.

Although the section focuses on the traditional in music, it is also forward-looking and it became the first section to insist on accepting only online entries. Any fears that this step would be resisted were groundless as numbers entering actually rose sharply.

Traditional music continues to thrive in Ballymena Festival and will keep on adapting and evolving.

# Modern Dance

Modern Dance is the newest discipline to join Ballymena Festival. The first competitions took place in 2014, with a newly formed committee being in charge of making all the arrangements. Modern Dance takes place at the end of the Festival, and it has quickly established itself in popularity. Many of those taking part come from all over Northern Ireland and the Modern Dance Committee members are delighted to be able to welcome them to the excellent facilities in The Braid.

The Committee for Modern Dance worked hard to ensure that the first year ran as smoothly as possible, being prepared to make adjustments in subsequent years. They also gathered support in the form of sponsorship or trophies from many local businesses and did everything they could to make the section as professional as possible - even though, like all Festival workers, they were volunteers.

A short history, then, in the context of the Festival's 100 years, but the presence of Modern Dance is indicative of the Festival organisers' wishes that the Festival would continue to be relevant and attractive to as many people as possible.

# APPENDIX C
## Trophies at Ballymena Festival

It would be an impossible task to catalogue all the trophies that have been presented to Ballymena Festival over its 100 years. The majority of the trophies are silver cups in various shapes and sizes, but there are also shields, an unusual silver potato ring, and a medallion in memory of Mary Wakefield.

Many of the trophies have been given in memory of those who have been involved with the festival in some capacity, ensuring that there remains a tangible link with them. A trophy will be retired from presentation if the class it was linked to no longer exists and if the wording on the trophy is so specific that it is impossible to link it to a different class. In such cases, the retired trophy is safely stored.

Some of the trophies that are presented have a long history and some even date back to the original Festival in 1916. These include

### The Shafto Adair Challenge Cup
This was originally presented to National School choirs (the equivalent of today's Primary Schools) and today is presented to the winners of Class 1, Primary School Choirs from the local Ballymena area.

### The J Dinsmore Cup
This was presented by Mr Dinsmore, husband of the founder of the Festival in Ballymena. It is currently presented to the winners of Class 2, Primary School choirs with no more than 100 pupils on the roll.

### The Hon Anne O'Neill Challenge Cup
This was awarded for piano and today is awarded for Class 109, open pianoforte solo.

### The Mary Wakefield Memorial Medallion
This dates back to 1916 and is in memory of one who may, with some justification, claim to have founded the competitive musical festival movement in rural areas in England. Mary Wakefield came from the Lake District and was passionate about the benefit of competitive music

festivals. She was the founder of the Association of Musical Competition Festivals, the forerunner of today's British and International Federation of Festivals of Music, Dance and Speech. The very first adjudicator in Ballymena, Dr W G McNaught, worked alongside Mary Wakefield before her death in 1912.

One of the most unusual trophies was presented to the Festival by Mr W Wier, husband of the long-time secretary, Ruth Wier, and the editor and proprietor of the Ballymena Observer. This is the Silver Potato Ring, originally designed to keep hot dishes away from varnished tables, and definitely not to store potatoes! It is currently awarded to the winner of Class 81, Irish Folk Song.

# APPENDIX D
## Ballymena Festival and the World Wide Web

When Ballymena Festival began in 1916, the idea of a computer would have seemed far-fetched. The notion of computers being able to communicate with each other would have been the stuff of science-fiction. It is probably difficult for modern children to imagine life devoid of computers and without access to the internet, but only a few years ago, administration in Ballymena Festival was carried out with pen and paper, perhaps stretching to the occasional typewriter. The manual paperwork system was extremely time-consuming for all concerned and an enormous burden for those secretaries with large numbers of entries.

In 2005, Dr Andrew Hudson realised that the management of the syllabus and the final Festival programme could be accomplished using a database of class definitions and other data which changed little from year to year. Accordingly he wrote a Microsoft Access database programme which also enabled the vocal and instrumental music sections to link entries for the festival. Secretaries in other sections, perhaps more comfortable with what they knew, continued to use their manual paperwork systems.

However, in 2010 the Committee agreed that the Festival should have a presence on the internet and work began by Andrew Hudson to design a website that would be a one-stop shop for all Festival data. The public would be able to access information from the site and could download the syllabus and entry forms for the different sections. The secretaries for the different sections could enter performers as entry forms arrived and extensive functionality was developed to enable them to construct the final performance programme using specially designed timing formulae. This is turn could be downloaded in a form that could be sent to a printing company to produce the written programme that is sold to the audience members as they arrive at the venue.

Dr Hudson not only designed the website but had to undertake a training programme for the section secretaries, some of whom were more computer literate than others. He showed remarkable patience in guiding them through the various steps and was always willing to explain things and assist whenever difficulties arose. There was no doubt that the new system saved time and helped the festival to look much more professional.

The website continued to be modified to make things run smoothly, but the next big development came in 2013 when it became possible for performers or teachers to enter themselves or their pupils online. This new development also included the ability to pay using PayPal. Once the performance programme had been arranged by the section secretary and entered on the website, anyone who had entered online received an automatic e-mail notification of their individual timetable.

In its present form, the website manages all data for the different sections. This includes the classes and their entry requirements, the performance programme, publication of prize-winners, the printing of the syllabus, the programme, call sheets, adjudication sheets, and all the other management activities associated with festival preparation and administration.

# APPENDIX E
## Adjudicators

From its beginning in 1916, Ballymena Festival has prided itself on employing the best adjudicators possible, believing that the knowledge that they can impart to competitors is invaluable. Their job is not an easy one since it demands great technical expertise, intense concentration levels and the ability to communicate well with performers and audience alike. Ballymena has played host to some famous names over the years, including eminent musicians and well-known actors and poets. Here are some of their stories.

## Sir Hugh S Roberton

Hugh S Roberton acted as Vocal adjudicator in Ballymena in 1923 and 1924, also adjudicating in Elocution in 1924. He was born in Glasgow in 1874, the son of an undertaker. Aged 21, he became General Manager of Glasgow Tramway and Omnibus Company's funeral department, but his heart lay with music. He was self-taught but from an early age had indulged his love of singing in and conducting choirs. Some said that he had a genius for conducting 'since he evoked from his fingers the feeling for the natural expression of every song.'

After six years of conducting funerals, the young Hugh Roberton successfully applied to become choir director of the Toynbee House choir. This eventually evolved into the Glasgow Orpheus choir, made up of working class men, many of whom had a political interest in the labour movement. The choir, under Roberton's direction, became well-known throughout Britain and many other 'People's choirs' were formed out of admiration for their singing and also for their political ideals. Roberton himself, although a pacifist, gave concerts for the wounded during the 1st World War and a military surgeon remarked that 'never till then had he realised the healing power of music.'

Hugh Roberton, founder of the famous Glasgow Orpheus Choir
©CSG CIC Glasgow Museum and Libraries Collection,
The Mitchell Library, Special Collection

In April 1924, Ramsay McDonald became Prime Minister and invited the Glasgow Orpheus choir to perform at 10 Downing Street, in the presence of the then Duke and Duchess of York. Shortly afterwards, of course, in May 1924, Roberton was adjudicating in Ballymena. Two years later, the choir gave a performance at Balmoral for the royal family. Roberton was knighted in 1931 and he continued with his prolific composing and conducting career.

In 1941, the BBC provoked controversy by seeming to be unwilling to broadcast the Glasgow Orpheus choir because of Sir Hugh Roberton's professed pacifism. Churchill himself spoke up for him in the Commons, 'I see no reason to suppose that the holding of pacifist views would make him play flat.'

By 1950, Roberton took the hard decision to disband the choir, believing that he was too old to give the energetic direction necessary to sustain its high standards. He died two years later in Glasgow.

# Tyrone Guthrie

Tyrone Guthrie was born in 1900 in England to parents of Scottish and Irish descent. He was educated at Wellington College and Oxford University where he studied ancient history and philosophy. His major interest, though, had always been the theatre, and after graduation, he joined the Oxford Playhouse as an actor and assistant stage manager.

Acting roles were limited for Tyrone Guthrie because at six feet five inches his height was rather noticeable. In 1924 he joined the BBC, working initially in Belfast as a radio announcer, director and scriptwriter. He eventually also worked at the BBC in London, where he wrote plays for the radio. During the 1920s he had taken some leaves of absence in order to pursue his love of the theatre and for a period he directed productions at the Scottish National Theatre. Cast and stage personnel alike were highly motivated by his directorial style. He also came to Ballymena to adjudicate in the relatively young discipline of Verse Speaking and Dramatic Interpretation.

He moved on to Cambridge as director of the Festival theatre, pioneering new stage techniques and acting styles, eventually moving to London to continue his directing career. A period of intense directing activity followed, bringing Guthrie more and more to the attention of not only the theatre world, but to the audiences who flocked to his innovative productions.

Tyrone Guthrie was a highly esteemed theatre and opera director

In 1946, Tyrone Guthrie entered the world of opera for the first time and was instrumental in reviving the fortunes of an art form that had suffered greatly during the war years. He was acclaimed at home and abroad for his imaginative productions of everything from opera to morality plays and during the 1940s and 1950s, his artistic vigour breathed new life into theatrical and opera classics.

Tyrone Guthrie was knighted in 1961, but he remained a down to earth man with simple tastes. He continued to direct and produce plays throughout the 1960s but eventually died in 1971 in his mother's ancestral home in Newbliss, Co Monaghan.

# Laurence Binyon

Laurence Binyon was the last adjudicator in
Speech and Drama before the outbreak of war in 1939

Robert Laurence Binyon was born in Lancashire in 1869, educated at St Paul's School, London and graduated in Classics from Trinity College, Oxford. While at university, he won the Newdigate prize for poetry in 1891.

His early working life was spent at the British Museum, eventually becoming Keeper of Oriental Prints and Drawings. He moved in highly intellectual circles in London with poets and artists among his friends.

He wrote his most famous poem 'For the fallen' very early in the Great War and it was published in The Times in September 1914. Too old to fight in the war, Binyon volunteered to work as a medical orderly in France.

After the war, Binyon took up his work at the British Museum, writing extensively on Oriental art. He continued to write poetry as well, with his collected poems being published in 1931. In 1933, Binyon retired from the museum and was appointed to be Norton Professor of Poetry in Harvard from 1933-1934. His academic work continued in Oxford in 1939. He was already an old man when he adjudicated in Verse speaking in Ballymena. His academic ventures took him next to Athens where he became Professor of English Literature in 1940. War caught up with him again and he managed to escape Greece before the Nazi invasion.

Binyon continued to immerse himself in scholarship, publishing a translation of Dante's 'Divine Comedy' and was working on another book when he became ill and died following an operation. His death came in 1943. In 1985, Laurence Binyon was commemorated, along with 15 other Great War poets, on a memorial stone in Poets' Corner in Westminster Abbey.

# Dr Havelock Nelson

Havelock Nelson, influential musician in Northern Ireland
*Image courtesy of Studio Symphony Orchestra, Belfast*

Havelock Nelson was born in Cork in 1917. He was both scientist and musician, combining both in his university studies in Dublin. He studied music at the Royal Irish Academy of Music as well as medical science at Trinity College Dublin. His doctoral research, completed in 1941, was in bacteriology. During his time in Dublin, he founded the amateur Dublin Orchestral players in 1939 with the aim of training young players and conductors, providing public performances of their repertoire.

Havelock Nelson served as a bacteriologist with the RAF during the war years and then joined the BBC in Northern Ireland in 1947, working as accompanist, broadcaster and composer. He also founded the Studio Opera Group in the 1950s with the aim of providing local singers with the opportunity to sing opera. This laid the foundation for what later developed into Castleward Opera. He also founded the Studio Symphony Orchestra which continues to provide the opportunity for amateur musicians to play together at a very advanced level. Havelock Nelson was awarded the OBE in 1966 in recognition of his services to music in Northern Ireland.

In addition to his own music career, Havelock Nelson was keen to nurture local talent and was instrumental in encouraging the musical development of Barry Douglas, James Galway and Heather Harper. He was also a sought after adjudicator both at home and abroad and, of course, adjudicated in Ballymena a number of times. He was a hugely influential figure in music in Northern Ireland throughout his thirty years of service with the BBC.

Havelock Nelson died in Belfast in 1993.

# List of Adjudicators

| 1. INSTRUMENTAL MUSIC | | 2. VOCAL MUSIC | |
|---|---|---|---|
| 1916 | W G McNaught | 1916 | W G McNaught |
| 1917 | E N Hay | 1917 | W G McNaught |
| 1918 | E N Hay | 1918 | W G McNaught |
| 1919 | Dr Coward/Mrs Tweed | 1919 | Dr Coward |
| 1920 | F H Sawyer | 1920 | E Gordon Cleather |
| 1921 | Thomas Weaving | 1921 | Dan Price |
| 1922 | Frederick Austin | 1922 | Dr R R Terry |
| 1923 | Frederick Bonavia | 1923 | Hugh S Roberton/ Stanley Roper |
| 1924 | Julius Harrison | 1924 | Hugh S Roberton |
| 1925 | W G Whittaker | 1925 | E T Davies |
| 1926 | Percy Scholes | 1926 | Dr D Vaughan Thomas |
| 1927 | Arthur Collingwood | 1927 | Prof Granville Bantock |
| 1928 | F H Sawyer | 1928 | Harvey Green/Walker Robson |
| 1929 | Dr Albert C Tysoe | 1929 | Arthur Collingwood |
| 1930 | Arthur Collingwood | 1930 | George Dodds |
| 1931 | Felix Swinstead | 1931 | Edgar Bainton |
| 1932 | Dr E Markham-Lee | 1932 | Dr J F Staton/D T Yacamini |
| 1933 | T H Weaving | 1933 | D T Yacamini/Dr J F Staton |
| 1934 | T H Weaving | 1934 | T Armstrong/F Austin |
| 1935 | T F Dunhill | 1935 | Dr Percy Hull |
| 1936 | Yeaman Dodds | 1936 | Topliss Green |
| 1937 | T F Dunhill | 1937 | T F Dunhill/Dr Staton |
| 1938 | D T Yacamini | 1938 | G Shaw/J Farrington |
| 1939 | D T Yacamini | 1939 | Topliss Green |

### NO COMPETITIONS DURING SECOND WORLD WAR

| | | | |
|---|---|---|---|
| 1946 | D T Yacamini | 1946 | Joseph Lewis |
| 1947 | Dr S Northcote | 1947 | Dr S Northcote/Alec Redshaw |
| 1948 | Dr S Northcote | 1948 | Dr S Northcote/Kenneth Roberton |
| 1949 | Michael Head | 1949 | Ronald Biggs |
| 1950 | R Walker Robson | 1950 | Ronald Biggs |
| 1951 | Michael Head | 1951 | Alec Redshaw |
| 1952 | Dr G H Moody | 1952 | Dr Havelock Nelson |
| 1953 | Dr H Wiseman | 1953 | Dr Havelock Nelson |
| 1954 | Brian Boydell | 1954 | Helen Henschel |
| 1955 | Dr Eric Thiman | 1955 | Helen Henschel |
| 1956 | Brian Boydell | 1956 | Dr J E Hutchinson |
| 1957 | Michael Head | 1957 | Michael Head |
| 1958 | Arthur Reckless | 1958 | Arthur Reckless |
| 1959 | John Churchill | 1959 | John Churchill |

## 1. INSTRUMENTAL MUSIC

1960  John Churchill
1961  Leslie Regan
1962  Herrick Bunney
1963  Brian Boydell
1964  Dr Melville Cook
1965  Dr Melville Cook
1966  Douglas Hopkins
1967  Michael Head
1968  John Williams
1969  Noel Cox
1970  Dr Gordon Slater
1971  Derek Cantrell
1972  Dr David Clover
1973  Dr Havelock Nelson
1974  Dr Edgar Boucher
1975  Donald Cairns/J Kirkwood

1976  Arthur Rooke/
       Michael McGuffin
1977  William Young
1978  John Rankin/Roger Jarvis
1979  Dr Edgar Boucher
1980  Roger Jarvis
1981  Elizabeth Bicker
1982  Michael McGuffin/Alex Soutar
1983  Wallace Berry
1984  George McPhee
1985  Brian Boydell
1986  Alex Soutar
1987  Dr Philip Cranmer
1988  John Railton
1989  Dennis Townhill
1990  James Kirkwood
1991  David Patrick

1992  Noel Cox/L Pugh/D Byers

1993  Neville Turner
1994  Alison Walker-Moorcroft
1995  Ivor Baynon/Donal McCrisken
1996  Elizabeth Bicker
1997  Elizabeth Bicker
1998  Elizabeth Bicker
1999  Neville Turner
2000  Dr Christopher Wiltshire
2001  Richard Deering
2002  Dr Michael Ball
2003  Neville Turner
2004  Dr Christopher Wiltshire

## 2. VOCAL MUSIC

1960  John Churchill
1961  Leslie Regan
1962  Herrick Bunney
1963  Brian Boydell
1964  Dr Melville Cook
1965  Dr Melville Cook
1966  Douglas Hopkins
1967  Michael Head
1968  John Williams
1969  Noel Cox
1970  Dr Gordon Slater
1971  Derek Cantrell
1972  Dr David Clover
1973  J Murray Brown
1974  Frank Laning
1975  Donald Cairns/J
       Kirkwood
1976  Arthur Rooke

1977  George McVicar
1978  John Rankin
1979  Wallace Berry
1980  Roger Jarvis
1981  George McVicar
1982  Alex Soutar
1983  Wallace Berry
1984  George McPhee
1985  Brian Boydell
1986  Alex Soutar
1987  Dr Philip Cranmer
1988  John Railton
1989  Dennis Townhill
1990  James Kirkwood
1991  Robin Hewitt/William
       Livingstone
1992  Noel Cox/William
       Livingstone
1993  Dr Harry Grindle
1994  Michael McGuffin
1995  James Wyld
1996  T Gwynn Jones
1997  James Kirkwood
1998  Marilynne Davies
1999  Jean Graham
2000  Vivien Pike
2001  Barbara Lowe
2002  Marilynne Davies
2003  Jean Graham
2004  Angela Feeney/M
       Powney

## 1. INSTRUMENTAL MUSIC
2005  Dr Michael Ball

2006  Richard Deering
2007  Marilynne Davies
2008  Elizabeth Bicker
2009  Dr Christopher Wiltshire

2010  Caroline Diffley
2011  Marilynne Davies
2012  Stuart Smith
2013  Helen Deakin
2014  Kay Tucker
2015  Robert Bailey
2016  Marilynne Davies

## 2. VOCAL MUSIC
2005  Margaret Duckworth/
      Angela Feeney
2006  Margaret Marsden
2007  Eileen Field
2008  Margaret Duckworth
2009  M Hancock/J
      Anderson
2010  Gaynor Keeble
2011  Marilynne Davies
2012  Maria Jagusz
2013  Eileen Field
2014  Nicola-Jane Kemp
2015  Christopher Field
2016  Marilynne Davies

## 3. SPEECH AND DRAMA
1924  Hugh S Roberton
1925  Mrs E Acton Bond
1926  Miss Katie Thomas
1927  Tyrone Guthrie
1928  Tyrone Guthrie
1929  Miss Rutherford Crockett
1930  Miss Rutherford Crockett
1931  Daniel Roberts
1932  Daniel Roberts
1933  Guy Pertwee
1934  Tyrone Guthrie
1935  Frank Ridley
1936  Harold Ripper
1937  Frank Ridley
1938  Kathleen Stone
1939  Lawrence Binyon

**NO COMPETITIONS DURING THE SECOND WORLD WAR**

1946  Dorothy Dayus
1947  Daniel Roberts
1948  Marjorie Lyon
1949  Daniel Roberts
1950  Nicholson Robson
1951  Miss Ray Ormonde
1952  Mr W J E Dawson
1953  Mrs M Kay
1954  Mrs M Kay
1955  Dorothy Watts
1956  Marjorie Lyon
1957  John Holgate
1958  Daniel Roberts
1959  Daniel Roberts
1960  Mrs H V Taggart
1961  William Bennett

### 3. SPEECH AND DRAMA

1962  Christobel Burniston
1963  Christobel Burniston
1964  W R S Bennett
1965  W R S Bennett
1966  Mrs H E Taggart
1967  Mrs H E Taggart
1968  Miss Stella Sizer-Simpson
1969  Barbara Macrea
1970  Barbart Macrea
1971  John Holgate
1972  Rona Blair
1973  Robert Freeburn
1974  W R S Bennett
1975  Christine Phillimore
1976  Jeanne Pells
1977  Margaret Tomlinson
1978  Silvie Taylor
1979  Ambrose Marriott
1980  Robert Freeburn
1981  Margaret Tomlinson
1982  Rona Laurie/Sally Noble
1983  Penelope Charteris
1984  Rona Laurie
1985  Ambrose Marriott
1986  Margaret Tomlinson
1987  Sally Noble/Ambrose Marriott
1988  Penelope Charteris/Stella Northover
1989  Paul Peters/Arthur Webb
1990  Silvie Taylor/W McKay Kenny
1991  Arthur Webb/Pat Mulligan
1992  Hilary Clulow/John McCavert
1993  Margaret Tomlinson/May McHenry
1994  Sally Noble
1995  Tom Martin
1996  Joan Skipper/Pat Mulligan
1997  Ann Warr
1998  Peggy Batchelor
1999  June Rayner
2000  Ann Warr
2001  David Fonville
2002  Anna Farmer
2003  Judy Buchanan
2004  Silvie Taylor
2005  Margaret Tomlinson
2006  Sue Mackay
2007  Carol Shroder
2008  Anna Farmer
2009  Aiden Crawley-Dynan
2010  Pat Mulligan
2011  Tish Nicholl
2012  Norma Redfearn

## 3. SPEECH AND DRAMA
2013  Maeve O'Donoghue
2014  Audrey Behan
2015  Sue Mackay
2016  Tish Nicoll

## 4. TRADITIONAL MUSIC
1961  Joe O'Dowd/Sean O'Driscoll
1963  K Harrington/J Keenan
1964  Sean O'Driscoll
1965  Sean O'Driscoll
1966  Felix Kearney
1967  Mr McNaughten
1968  Frank Hickenbottom
1969  Frank Hickenbottom
1970  Frank Hickenbottom/Sean O'Driscoll
1971  Sean O'Driscoll
1972  Tony Smith
1974  John Mawhinney/D McCavanagh
1979  Denis Sweeney/John Hendy
1981  P Ryan/Art McNally
1982  Tony Smith/Art McNally
1983  Michael MacAogain
1984  G Egan/M O'Laughlin
1985  Michael Aogain
1986  Tony Smith/Art McNally
1987  Michael Aogain
1988  M ni Lochlan/M Aogain/Art McNally
1989  F O'Rahilly/Tony Smith
1990  Art McNally
1991  F O'Rahilly/Tony Smith
1992  Tony Smith
1993  Tony Smith
1994  Art McNally
1995  Sean Maguire/Maeve McKeown
1996  Dick Glasgow
1997  Amy Geddis
1998  Padraig O'Brien
1999  Brian McAteer
2000  Clodagh Warnock
2001  Wilbert Garvin
2002  Ron Stewart/Jim Faulkener
2003  Wilbert Garvin/Barbara Grey
2004  Colm Murphy
2005  John Duffin
2006  Michael Brown
2007  James Byrne/Maeve McKeown
2008  Niall McClean
2009  Laura Beagon
2010  John Duffin
2011  Colin McAllister
2012  Eithne Vallely

## 4. TRADITIONAL MUSIC
2013  Niall McClean
2014  Martin Donohoe
2015  Siobhan Molloy
2016  Brid Harper

## 5. BALLET
1948  Mrs D Marshall
1949  Mrs D Hardy
1950  Miss Kelly
1951  Mrs D Marshall
1952  Miss L Hainsworth

## 6. MODERN DANCE
2014  Gayle Johnson
2015  Jodie Clarke

## 7. TRADITIONAL DANCE
1929  Dennis Cuffe
1930  Sean O'Donohoe
1931  Risdeard MacGabhann
1932  Risdeard MacGabhann
1933  Peadar O'Rafferty
1934  Frank Roche
1935  Frank Roche
1936  Peadar O'Rafferty/J Quigley/Miss Mulholland
1937  George Leonard
1938  George Leonard
1939  George Leonard

## NO COMPETITIONS DURING SECOND WORLD WAR

1946  Sean O'Quigley
1947  Frank Higginson
1948  G O'Rafferty
1949  G O'Rafferty
1950  Sean O'Rafferty
1951  R F Smyth
1952  R F Smyth
1953  George Leonard
1954  George Leonard
1955  George Leonard/Patrick Ferguson
1956  Mona Scully
1957  Mona Scully/Patrick Ferguson
1958  Kevin McKenna/Anna Richmond
1960  Mona Scully/Eamonn Murray
1961  Mr R F Roddy
1962  Mr G Hobbs
1963  George Leonard
1964  Mona Scully
1965  Patrick Kinder
1966  J F Brown

## 7. TRADITIONAL DANCE

1967  Patrick Kinder
1968  J F Brown
1969  Mrs V Black
1970  Patrick Kinder
1971  Philip Carroll
1972  Mrs Mamie Graham
1973  Irene McCann
1974  Mrs Rowles
1975  Mary Timlin
1977  Irene McCann
1978  Sally Tanner
1979  Catriona Crilly
1980  Kathleen Skeffington
1981  Mrs Mamie Graham
1982  Geoffrey McNabb
1983  Irene McCann
1984  E F McCanny
1985  Mrs G Mulligan
1987  Silvia Rice
1988  Niall McCullough
1989  Brian Laverty
1990  Mrs G Mulligan
1991  Silvia Rice
1992  Judith McCormick
1994  Mrs M Gardiner
1995  Patricia Havelin/Tony Fox
1996  Margaret Wray/Paddy Dillon/Karina McCollum
1997  Martin McToal/Leslie Baird
2001  Siobhan Meban/Denise Dobbin/Gillian Blair
2007  Stacey Maguire
2008  Irene McCann
2009  Deborah Anderson
2010  J McLester/E Cunningham
2011  Orla McIntyre/Stacey Maguire
2012  Gillian Armstrong
2013  Leslie Baird
2014  Laura Mills
2015  David Barkley
2016  Marlene Oliver

Please note that there are names missing in the lists of adjudicators; however the lists are as complete as possible.